What is
Political Sociology?

What is Sociology? series

Elisabeth S. Clemens, *What is Political Sociology?*
Hank Johnston, *What is a Social Movement?*
Richard Lachmann, *What is Historical Sociology?*

What is
Political Sociology?

ELISABETH S. CLEMENS

polity

First published in 2016 by Polity Press

Polity Press
65 Bridge Street
Cambridge CB2 1UR, UK

Polity Press
350 Main Street
Malden, MA 02148, USA

ISBN-13: 978-0-7456-9160-2
ISBN-13: 978-0-7456-9161-9(pb)

A catalogue record for this book is available from the British Library.

Library of Congress Cataloging-in-Publication Data

Names: Clemens, Elisabeth Stephanie, 1958- author.
Title: What is political sociology? / Elisabeth S. Clemens.
Description: Malden, MA : Polity Press, [2016] | Includes bibliographical
   references and index.
Identifiers: LCCN 2016003611| ISBN 9780745691602 (hardcover :
   alk. paper) | ISBN 0745691609 (hardcover : alk. paper) | ISBN
   9780745691619 (pbk. : alk. paper) | ISBN 0745691617
   (pbk. : alk. paper)
Subjects: LCSH: Political sociology.
Classification: LCC JA76 .C5385 2016 | DDC 306.2–dc23 LC record
   available at http://lccn.loc.gov/2016003611

Typeset in 10.5 on 12 pt Sabon
by Toppan Best-set Premedia Limited
Printed and bound in the UK by Clays Ltd, St Ives PLC

For further information on Polity, visit our website: politybooks.com

Contents

Acknowledgments

I am grateful to Richard Lachmann, Ann Shola Orloff, and Jonathan Skerrett for generative conversations about the shape of this project. The students in "Political Sociology" during Autumn 2014 provided a challenging audience for the first run through the argument; Jeffrey Parker and Jae Ahn Wan carefully watched what worked and what didn't in the class assignments. Colleagues and graduate students in the Politics/History/Society workshop at the University of Chicago provided valuable and constructive critique of the conceptual framework, while the gift of a fellowship year at the Center for Advanced Study in the Behavioral Sciences afforded the time and good company to revise the manuscript without the press of everyday duties. The final manuscript has benefited greatly from the comments of two anonymous reviewers as well as an insightful and incisive reading from Cedric de Leon.

Introduction

With an entire discipline devoted to political science, what is distinctive about political sociology? One clue can be found in the fact that many political scientists – those at Harvard, University of Texas, Georgetown, and the London School of Economics, among others – actually teach in departments of *government*. While there is not a bright line between political science and political sociology, the former typically focuses on the formal institutions and acts of governing. Political sociology, by contrast, expands the field of view to explore the politics that happens in other social settings – in the family, at work, in civic associations – as well as the ways in which social relations and attributes shape patterns of political participation and the distribution of political power. How does voting vary by class, gender, ethnicity and race, education, or religion? What sorts of people are most likely to exercise political power? And to what ends?

This expansive focus is informed by a particular sense of the political – or, perhaps more accurately, the "politicized" (Fraser 1990: 204) – that is contrasted with settled relationships within or between domains of social life. Politics can happen within the workplace or the family, when established routines, taken-for-granted goals, or accepted authority relationships are unsettled and contested. Politics can also happen between domains of social life, as when wives entered into paid labor, raising a question of whether their wages would be governed by the rules accepted in workplaces about the worker's ownership of their labor or by the norms that governed family life in the nineteenth century in which husbands had claims to much of their wives' property. A particularly potent form of politics occurs at the boundaries of established political institutions, as the excluded seek access and the established seek to preserve their advantages. For sociologists, politics happens in any setting where people come to grasp the connections between biography and history or personal troubles and public issues, connections that C. Wright Mills understood as central to the "sociological imagination" (1959: 6). Politics, in this broad sociological sense, may ultimately play out in institutions that are officially designated as "political" and widely accepted as the places – courts, legislatures, elections – where important questions of law, policy, and distribution should be decided.

But those institutions, which are often imagined as housed in white marble buildings or imposing official compounds, are also subject to sociological analysis. Such institutions are not pure realizations of the designs of political theorists or constitutional architects, but have been built up through systems of social relations and cultural understanding, themselves often appropriated from other domains of social life. As a consequence, political sociology does not simply ask how political institutions work, but how they are constructed, with what consequences, and with what potential for significant change and transformation?

These questions establish an expansive agenda for political sociology, so it is helpful to begin by settling on a basic set of concepts and lines of analysis. Chapter 1 takes on this task, exploring how the dynamics of social caging and social closure help us to think about the emergence of states as well as the contrast between the relations of direct and indirect rule. As distinctive kinds of political institutions are built out of various combinations of social networks, different frameworks for political action emerge. These set the terms within which individuals decide to participate, acquiesce to authority, or mobilize in opposition. The effects of all these decisions are, in turn, embodied in law, policy, and practices that shape the constitution of political selves, interests, and ideologies, thereby structuring the next round of political action.

The contrast between direct and indirect forms of rule illuminates the key differences between two political forms that have dominated much of global political history: empires and nation-states. As chapter 2 details, the differences between these types of political order raise questions about why states take varied forms. Shared cultural identities coincide with political order in some cases but not in others. By focusing on the centrality of shared identity as a "people" in distinguishing empires and nation-states, this analysis also documents how culture operates within nation-states through patterns of belief, practices of discipline, and the constitution of political subjects who may be more or less susceptible to centralized rule.

If some political transformations are generated by tensions within transnational or imperial systems, others are fueled by relations of domination, exclusion, and exploitation within relatively bounded political orders. Chapter 3 addresses these dynamics of political change, focusing on the sociology of revolution and the question, as posed by Barrington Moore (1966), of what drove some countries on the road to democracy or to dictatorship. Before turning to the first of those paths for an extended consideration of democratic politics, this chapter concludes with a consideration of the totalitarian alternative as a system of social relations and organizational forms.

With chapters 4 and 5, there is an explicit narrowing of scope. The focus shifts to political dynamics within modern democratic polities. Political sociologists have approached questions of democratic participation and the "democratic state" from two opposed directions. Research on political socialization and participation has tended to begin with the individual in order to understand overall outcomes as aggregations of the preferences, decisions, and acts of a great many citizens. Chapter 4 surveys these arguments, exploring how social contexts and relationships are incorporated into "bottom-up" models which take individual behavior as an "input" and policy as an "output." Chapter 5 then reverses perspective, presenting arguments that begin with the character and organization of "the state." The varying relationships between "state and society," including policies that delimit the electorate and policy feedbacks that influence individual preferences represent important approaches to the ways in which "policy shapes politics."

Once a democratic – or even partially democratic – polity is constructed, opposition can mobilize through political channels. But official institutions cannot always contain protest and address grievances. In many cases, people choose to pursue their grievances and advance their demands outside the channels of institutional politics, through social movements and other projects of social change. Chapter 6 reviews the major arguments in these literatures, exploring how they expand our understanding of political socialization or the biographical impact of movement participation as well as processes of regime change, picking up on themes from the earlier discussion of the sociology of revolution.

Political change can lead in many directions, to democracy or dictatorship or other already familiar ways of organizing power. For centuries, empire and nation-state emerged from, reinforced, and sometimes destabilized the other model for political order. Chapter 7 addresses the possibilities for new trajectories of political change driven by the interaction of national and transnational developments. Some observers have claimed that globalization is fundamentally unraveling – or perhaps re-scaling – the social cages that we know as nation-states. To what extent have such processes exposed or aggravated the incapacity of nation-states to manage political conflict and reflection? When and where have political actors succeeded in constructing new, if partial, forms of political ordering using social materials that are creatively repurposed and recombined? The answers to such questions about the possible futures of political order begin with a turn to its past, the emergence of durable forms of organized power.

1
Power and Politics

Travel through almost any part of the world and many of the must-see sites are the physical traces of political orders long gone: castles along the Rhine, the Great Wall of China, the expansive temple complexes of Central America, North Africa, and Southeast Asia, or even a cluster of stone-walled granaries on a windswept plateau in the American Southwest. Each of these places embodies some method for enhancing the ability of human beings to control their environment, to produce collective goods, and, almost always, for some to dominate others. European castles were simultaneously centers of economic activity, "seats" of power that linked family dynasties to recognized and legitimate rule, and military resources that anchored a zone of security and exploitation across a surrounding region. The formal political authority of the ruler who occupied such a castle was rooted in a wider web of social and economic activities as well as shared sets of cultural and religious meanings. Although in very different ways, the same was true of the emperors who built the Great Wall, the priests who controlled those temples, or the locally recognized leaders of any small human group only a few centuries removed from subsistence through hunting and gathering.

Almost any given place has been shaped by the layering of different ways of organizing power. If you were to begin from those rough stone granaries in the southeast corner of Utah, you would start in a place settled by multiple Native American societies, then claimed as territory by the United States when it defeated Mexico (formerly a colony of Spain), organized as a theocracy by Mormon settlers who were then forced to change their laws to conform to demands by the US Congress in order to enter into statehood. A looping, clockwise tour around the Four Corners – defined by right angles on a map drawn thousands of miles to the east in Washington DC, with the east–west boundary reflecting a hoped-for compromise between free and slave states in the national legislature – would take you through contemporary tribal reservations that are simultaneously sovereign entities and subject to the federal government, past the ruins of Chaco Canyon at the heart of a great regional system a thousand or more years ago, through regions taken from Spain by war, from an independent Mexico by yet more war, and from an independent Mexico by purchase. Each of these paths to a new form of political order was, in turn, shaped by systems of trade, rules about property ownership, spiritual practices, and family systems.

A similarly complex tour through the archaeology of power could be charted for almost any part of the world. The United Kingdom is precisely that: an agglomeration of the separate kingdoms of England, Wales, later Scotland, and then a portion of Ireland once ruled by yet other kings. Both Italy and Germany are modern nation-states constructed out of a wondrous variety of principalities, duchies, free cities, and other types of political order that have fallen out of regular use. Modern India, Pakistan, and Bangladesh encompass lands held separately by a great many dynasties, aggregated by the British Empire and then divided into first two, and then three, independent nation-states. The innumerable ways in which power is socially organized are evident in both these legacies from the past and in any contemporary system of political power with its military bases, border fences and checkposts, national museums or memorials, and the free trade zones and tariffs that structure international economic ties and protect domestic industries.

The organization of power is shaped by, and acts back upon, the places, buildings, and processes that we usually designate as "political": grand government buildings, sessions of Congress or Parliament, campaign debates, and voting practices. Whereas political scientists often begin with questions about the workings and consequences of these elements of formal government (e.g. the legislative, the executive, the judiciary), political sociologists start from puzzles about why power is organized in one way rather than another, questions that usually require expanding our field of vision to think about the relationship of formal politics to economic conflicts, religious beliefs, family practices, and a wide range of social identities. Castle, Great Wall, temple complex, and cluster of granaries – each of these represents a distinctive way of constructing political order out of the material of social life.

The variation across these sites poses the central question for political sociology: How can we explain the emergence, reproduction, and transformation of different forms of political ordering? Because political sociology grapples with these issues across an enormous range of historical and geographic settings, from the intimate relations that constitute family politics to the geopolitical scales of war and trade, the first requirement is to assemble the most helpful conceptual toolkit. And there is no more important place to begin than with the concept of power.

Understanding Power

For political sociologists, the German social theorist Max Weber (1864–1920) provided the classic definition of power (or *Macht* in the original) as "the probability that one actor within a social relationship will be in a position to carry out his own will despite resistance, regardless of the basis on which this probability rests" (Weber 1978 [1918–20]: 58). At first glance, this definition seems to provide little leverage. It is like turning to a dictionary to understand a word that you have used in conversation for years only to find a definition that restates your uncertainty. But, when one looks at the definition from a different perspective, asking what it assumes and what conditions must exist for "power" to be possible, more interesting questions can be posed.

First, notice that the exercise of power requires a differentiation of preferences. One actor's "will" must be distinct from that of another actor. In Weber's sense, there is no power in a hive or "borg," where multiple actors act as one, sharing the same instincts, desires, and strategic goals. This imagery evokes Emile Durkheim's (1857–1917) concept of "mechanical solidarity," "which comes from a certain number of states of conscience which are common to all members of the same society" (1964 [1933]: 109). This form of solidarity was most pronounced, according to Durkheim, in those early forms of human society that were not marked by a well-developed division of labor with its specialization of activities and relations of interdependence among members. To the extent that processes of social and economic differentiation were central to the analyses of modernity advanced by the founding generation of sociological theorists, these classic arguments are also accounts of the emergence of the conditions for the exercise and institutionalization of power. As Alexis de Tocqueville (1805–59) noted in the introduction to his classic *Democracy in America*, one could look back over centuries of European history and view the appearance of divides between clergy and crown, the emergence of a judiciary and a merchant class as simply the multiplication of "new avenues to power" (2004: 4).

Second, the exercise of power rests on an uneven distribution of resources or the ability to influence others "despite resistance." In a social world where all actors are fundamentally equal, a series of one-to-one conflicts can generate a hierarchy or "pecking order" only to have those relations of domination upended by the next encounter. So just as classic social and political theorists – from John Locke to Karl Marx – often began with questions about the origins of property, an adequate political sociology must address the question of the sources of significant and durable inequality in the capacity to dominate others.

Finally, Weber's definition of power presumes that those upon whom power is exercised do not have the option of exit. They must stay and take it, when another actor imposes his or her own will on them. Challenging early modern political theorists who sought to derive political authority from natural inequalities among individuals, Jean-Jacques Rousseau (1712–78) acknowledged that one person "might seize the fruits which another had gathered, the game he had killed, or the cave he had chosen for shelter; but how would he ever be able to exact obedience, and what ties of dependence could there be among men without possessions?" Imagining himself at the mercy of such a person, Rousseau noted that "he must bind me fast before he goes to sleep, or I shall certainly either knock him on the head or make my escape ... let him but turn his head aside at any sudden noise, and I shall be instantly twenty paces off, lost in the forest, and, my fetters burst asunder, he would never see me again" (1959: 232–3). Power, for both Weber and Rousseau, ends at the point where an individual rejects domination in order to escape into the forest, or away across the windswept mesa, or into the regions beyond the Great Wall.

These three conditions for power – at least as Weber understood it – are met when a particular kind of social order is in place, one that combines social differentiation (in terms of both a division of labor and a cultural understanding of individuals as distinct and self-determining), relatively durable patterns of inequality or social rank, and some boundary between membership in that order and the unsettled world beyond that basic social group – the forest, the hills, the wilderness. In many early social groupings, that boundedness was not physically marked but was produced by the benefits of remaining a part of the collective rather than venturing out alone. Those stone granaries in southern Utah represented a technology for storing food, strategically placed near springs, in places that could be defended against marauders, both human and animal. To leave the group that controlled such places involved accepting full reliance on oneself alone for survival. But to benefit from the collectively produced benefits of stored food, access to water, and a degree of security required some subordination of an individual's will to those of others. In this way, any dependence on cooperation with or support from others increases the cost of exit and provides an opportunity for the exercise of power. The durable organization of power rests on what sociologist Michael Mann (1986) has termed a "social cage."

Social Cages and Social Closure

When thinking of fortified castles and walled cities, "social cage" seems an appropriate description. But in what sense can this concept provide a more general foundation for political sociology? According to Mann, a social cage involves "the containment of human beings behind clear, fixed, confined social and territorial boundaries" (1986: 38). In its most important historical forms, such containment produces insulation from uncertainty through ritual, insulation from time through writing and other cultural practices of memorialization, and insulation from the outside through the concentration of individuals in towns and cities. Tracing a long prehistory of power through the Neolithic revolution (the appearance of agriculture and the domestication of animals) and early settlements, the archaeological record provides considerable evidence of inequality or "ranked" societies in varied grave goods and ritual artifacts. But for inequality to be transformed into a "social cage" requires the "conversion of temporary authority into permanent coercive power" (1986: 100). In Mann's reading of the research literature, this only occurs with the development of more extensive forms of the division of labor, above all irrigation systems, and the unequal distribution of the products of such a division of labor.

Imagine what it would be like to get the short end of the stick in such a society. Whereas Rousseau could picture himself whacking his captor on the head to escape back into the forest, you would be faced with the choice between taking a smaller share of the harvest or giving up any share in order to leave the settlement and venture into the hills on your own. Although the specifics differ, dissidents in East Germany in 1989 had to make a comparable choice (see chapter 3): stay in a place where they had social networks and promises of public services or attempt to cross into Western Europe with the risks of a very uncertain future. The extent to which our own lives are constituted by and within social cages is the stuff of dystopian novels. When the electricity fails, when law enforcement disintegrates, when shipments of food do not appear on store shelves, we see the extent to which the quality of our individual lives has rested on complex webs of inter-dependence. As such grim fictions of a possible future make clear, the benefits of participating in a more advanced division of labor make escape more costly. Recall Rousseau's question: "What ties of dependence could there be among men without possessions?" Collective efforts at production and the resulting ties of dependence create the conditions for durable relations of power.

The construction of durable systems of power wasn't easy or automatic. Absent extreme inequalities of property and resources (including the physical strength of individual bodies), any would-be tyrant might be toppled by a combination of two or more others who refused to submit. The same skills and tools that were developed for early forms of agricultural or artisanal production could be carried away by a group who decided that they would prefer to leave for the hills rather than remain to be dominated by others. So, according to Mann, durable relations of power tended to emerge in places where the benefits of sustained cooperation were particularly high or the costs of exit particularly daunting. River valleys, such as the Nile or the Indus, bordered by desert or mountains, exemplify ecologies that first made possible "the closing of the escape route" (Mann 1986: 75). Complete closure, of course, is almost impossible. The same river valleys that increase the costs of exit are also transit corridors, embedding any given center of settlement in flows of migration, trade, fashion, and war. But variation in the costs of "exit" (a concept we will consider later in this chapter) produces changing opportunities for the consolidation of orderings based on power.

Once those escape routes become less accessible, new dynamics develop. Those who benefit from a division of labor through the exercise of power may organize to protect their advantages. Similarly, those who get the short end of the stick – or the smaller share of the harvest – may begin to talk among themselves, to rally together, to threaten, in order to shift the distribution of benefits. These processes represent another basic concept of political sociology: social closure. Explaining the emergence of systems of "durable inequality," sociologist Charles Tilly (1929–2008) appealed to Weber: "the creation of what [Weber] called 'social closure' advanced efforts by the powerful to exclude less powerful people from the full benefits of joint enterprises, while facilitating efforts by underdogs to organize for the seizure of benefits denied" (1998: 6–7). Operating on the principle that "the enemy of my enemy is my friend" (a version of what sociologists call "structural equivalence"), those who lose out in relations of exploitation have a possible incentive to join together to change the terms of the division of labor.

In order to protect or even increase their advantages, elites may construct a social form that we know as "the state": "a differentiated set of institutions and personnel embodying centrality, in the sense that political relations radiate outward to cover a territorially demarcated area, over which it claims a monopoly of binding and permanent rule-making, backed up by physical violence" (Mann 1986: 37). As new arrangements increase the ability of some to exploit and dominate others, social hierarchy becomes more intense and, potentially, more secure. As elites come to control a greater share of the collective capacity of their communities, they may use this to extend the scope of their domination, bringing new villages and regions into a system of organized power (Tilly 1992: 24–5).

The outcome of collective action to preserve, increase, or contest the existing division of labor or distribution of benefits will depend in large part on the social networks available for mobilization. "Social closure" points to the many ways in which social ties and networks contribute to the organization of power. Kinship or family ties have been particularly important for early efforts at state-making (Adams 1994). Powerful families may require their sons and daughters to marry into other powerful lineages. This linking of family and the advantages of wealth or status constitutes a kind of hoarding of power that is reproduced across generations. Shared religious practices or ethnic backgrounds may be used to determine access into particular occupations or to condemn others to work in the least rewarding or respected activities. As Tilly notes, these inequalities may become embodied in the fullest sense. Across the British army and navy of the late eighteenth century, the officers were marked bodily as well as by uniforms and insignia: "an average beginning military cadet stood some 10 inches taller than a newly recruited mariner" (1998: 2). In studies of modern societies, greater earnings continue to be associated with height as well as beauty, straight teeth, nice clothes, and credentials from elite universities, all individual attributes that can be enhanced by higher family incomes. Even in electoral democracies, family ties can serve as political advantages, a point obvious not just to Americans in an era of Clintons and Bushes but also in the succession of Nehru and multiple Gandhis as leaders of the Congress Party in India, or the passing of the leadership of France's National Front party from father to daughter. In these ways, and many more, those who belong to advantaged social groups continually find new ways to defend their advantage and to ensure that it will be extended to their children and grandchildren.

Social closure may begin as small-scale clique formation, as mutual protection and aid among those who share kinship or location, social practices or religious beliefs. Such basic "us and them" structures, built on the interdependence of a division of labor or mutual defense, can then aggregate into more durable lines of categorical difference: civilized and barbarian, believer and infidel, members of distinctive peoples and races (Weber 1978 [1918–1920]: 385–98). These attributions of group difference may be anchored in perception of physiological difference – whether hairstyle or beards or skin color – but traits such as "race" create "a 'group' only when it is subjectively perceived as a common trait: this happens only when a neighborhood or the mere proximity of racially different persons is the basis of joint (mostly political) action, or conversely, when some common experiences of members of the same race are linked to some antagonism against members of an *obviously* different group" (Weber 1978 [1918–1920]: 385). Thus race, ethnicity, or any other categorical identity should not be understood as a pre-existing – much less primordial or natural – source of conflict, but rather as identities that "happen" through processes of conflict and competition. In some settings, cross-cutting identities may generate distinctive experiences of "intersectionality" (Cohen 1999; McCall 2005), while other intersections of identity categories may provide a framework for building alliances and coalitions (Heaney and Rojas 2015; Jung et al. 2014).

Such processes of closure along lines of kinship, ethnicity, religion, or class create new opportunities for the exercise and amassing of power by those who are able to build networks that cross-cut these social boundaries and to act as "brokers" at the intersection of different kinds of identity and loyalty. In a classic account of the emergence of a hierarchy of power out of overlapping networks, John Padgett and Christopher Ansell (1993) demonstrated how one of the great figures of Renaissance Florence – Cosimo de Medici – sat at the intersection of networks based on relations of marriage, co-residence in neighborhoods, debtor–creditor ties, and political sponsorship. By sitting at key intersections in the relations that structured everyday life for much of the Florentine elite, Cosimo accrued and benefitted from a distinctive form of influence: "Control is when others' locked-in interactions generate a flow of collective behavior that just happens to serve one's interests" without requiring one to engage in overt domination or to mobilize to advance one's self-interest (1993: 1259). A similar intuition, although grounded on different core theoretical assumptions, informs Pierre Bourdieu's (1930–2002) analysis of the emergence of the state. Bourdieu's analysis foregrounds state power "over the different fields and over the different particular species of capital, and especially over the rates of conversion between them (and thereby) over the relations of force between their respective holders)" (1994: 4). If society is understood as composed of multiple networks or fields, then control over the intersections and overlaps is an important source of power.

In addition to serving as a mechanism for the consolidation of elites and for the construction of control-through-brokerage, "social closure" can also be a means for contesting systems of inequality. Those who share a disadvantaged situation often find that their common experience can lead to mobilization, particularly when it is linked to shared religious beliefs or physical traits or occupational settings. Deploying what political scientist James Scott (1987) has described as the "weapons of the weak," peasants can contest and subvert the authority of the powerful, even to the point of mobilizing rebellions. In industrialized societies, Karl Marx (1818–83) traced a related process whereby the shared experience of exploitation in the unprecedentedly large factories of nine-teenth-century Britain would provoke workers to recognize one another as members of a group defined by their shared relation of exploitation by their employer. This formation of a group identity based on their common position in an industrial division of labor would, Marx predicted, fuel the transformations of workers from a "class in itself" (structural equivalence without shared identity or collective action) to a "class for itself." In this way, even the shared "immiseration" of poorly paid, de-skilled industrial workers could generate a new resource for contesting power in the form of a common identity, grievances, and capacity to act collectively (Tucker 1978: 473–83).

The concepts of social caging and social closure provide the foundation for a sociological approach to the study of politics. They illuminate how configurations of social relations constitute bounded social orders, generate patterns of group formation, and fuel conflict among groups. But in a world marked by inequality and social closure, we would expect to see constant conflict and contestation rather than the routine, settled, taken-for-granted, and even apathetic political life that is typical of many times and places. To explain the absence of conflict, despite difference and inequality, requires further elaboration of the concept of power.

The Dimensions of Power

Marx's theory predicts that shared experiences of exploitation will lead to group formation (social closure and the emergence of a shared identity) and then to collective political action. But the exertion of power over others often operates without ever producing politics in the sense of debate or conflict over the ordering of power. In a now-classic political ethnography, John Gaventa analyzed one such case. Looking at the profound poverty and misery of coal miners in Appalachia, he was puzzled why so much shared experience of exploitation by the powerful had produced so little political mobilization: "Why, in a social relationship involving the domination of a non-elite by an elite, does challenge to that domination not occur? What is there in certain situations of social deprivation that prevents issues from arising, grievances from being voiced, or interests from being recognized?" (Gaventa 1980: 4).

These questions led Gaventa to go beyond Weber's definition of power and its presumption of two actors in direct relation to one another. For Weber, wills differ. One actor successfully influences the other, "despite resistance." In some cases, however, this direct influence may not be needed. A second level or "face" of power is at play when the exercise of power takes the form of controlling access to the decision or political debate in the first place (Bachrach and Baratz 1962; Lukes 1974). So a particularly wealthy or well-connected Athenian may have exerted power in Weber's first sense over a less advantaged citizen, but both citizens together exerted power in the second sense over the women and slaves and foreigners who were forbidden to participate in political deliberations. This control over access to the political may also be exercised with respect to issues. In the early nineteenth century, successive majorities in the US Congress imposed a "gag rule," which prevented legislative consideration of the great many petitions for the abolition of slavery that were submitted by citizens. In the decades after the Civil War, the leadership of both the Democratic and Republican parties worked to keep questions of woman suffrage and temperance out of party platforms, fearing that they would split the different cross-regional coalitions upon which each party depended. In increasingly complex political systems, it is possible to avoid the need to exert direct influence over someone else by preventing the divisive issue from ever coming to a debate or a vote.

As Gaventa considered the puzzle of political quiescence in Appalachia, however, neither of these explanations seemed adequate. It wasn't that miners were losing votes in the state legislatures or that they were agitating for the governor to address their grievances. They were simply quiet. The experience of misery and exploitation had become so familiar that it had come to seem inevitable, even natural and possibly necessary. Just as the greater height of those British officers made them appear destined for command over their short-statured soldiers and sailors, so the vastly different circumstances of elites and miners could be understood as expressing some deeper, ordained social order. What may have seemed inevitable to miners, however, was assiduously produced and reinforced by mine owners and their allies in the press, by many preachers in the pulpits, and by the admonitions of social workers and government bureaucrats.

Gaventa's argument underscores the importance of considering all the dimensions of power that are at play in the construction of social cages and processes of social closure. For those who are advantaged by some particular arrangement, it is helpful to make that arrangement seem inevitable, natural, even divinely ordained. Thus kings are anointed by bishops to harness the force of religious faith to a system of rule just as ardent Jacksonian democrats in the early nineteenth century insisted that women, African Americans, and Native Americans were so obviously dependent and childlike that they were unfit to exercise the vote. A critical form of political mobilization, therefore, is precisely criticism itself or the work of exposing the non-naturalness of relationships of power. But even were relationships of power to be fully and completely exposed, each actor would still be left facing a classic political question: What is to be done? Submit, stand and fight, or run into the forest?

Exit, Voice, and Loyalty

Political sociology bridges a seeming contradiction. The organization of power is the product of relationships of constraint, exploitation, and exclusion: social cages and social closure. Yet politics itself requires a kind of freedom, the capacity to imagine that systems of power and inequality could be organized differently. Since all actors, even those who are relatively advantaged, are caught up in networks of dependence on others, all face a question about how to respond to perceived grievances and sources of constraint.

A leading economist of development, Albert O. Hirschman (1915–2012), provided a powerful lens for thinking about this question. His own selections among these options shaped his biography as he chose to leave a German university to fight on the republican side in the Spanish Civil War, then helped refugees fleeing Nazi-occupied France, and finally served in the US Army and Office of Strategic Services. Faced with an unsatisfactory situation, he argued, individuals could take one of three paths: loyalty, or continuing as before despite dissatisfaction; voice, or an effort to engage with the source of dissatisfaction in order to improve the situation; or exit. In a rough sense, these line up with the options available to Rousseau's man held captive: Submit, stand and fight, or run into the forest?

As Gaventa understood when he tried to understand the quiescence of those Appalachian miners, loyalty is an exceptionally strong source of stability for political orders. Loyalty can take strong and ideologically articulate forms such as "my country, right or wrong" or come closer to something inarticulate such as habit. This is just where we are and how we do politics. Loyalty may be grounded in cultural beliefs but also reinforced by the provision of services and adoption of policies that conform to the preferences of political subjects. Whether loyalty is to a particular person or to an understanding of "how things are here," such an embrace of the status quo can depoliticize people despite their grievances or lead them to mobilize in support of a regime notwithstanding all its faults.

Exit can also contribute to either stabilization or change, depending on the balance between the disappearance of critics and the evaporation of key portions of the population on which a political order depends. It is no coincidence that exile has been a political tool for rulers, a way of banishing critics from ongoing conversations about the legitimacy of a particular ruler or regime. Those disappointed and disillusioned by exit may also engage in a kind of internal exile, failing to exercise their vote even though they are formally entitled to participate in elections. In the chapters that follow, both loyalty and exit will figure as important mechanisms for the reproduction and transformation of political orders.

But politics – and political sociology – focuses on the exercise of voice, particularly when it comes to understanding contemporary democratic societies. Analytically, "voice" comprises political speech and action, whether in the course of peacefully assembling to protest, or participating in the routines of electoral democracy, or simply debating issues of public concern over the dinner table, among friends, or on the bus. The specific arenas and practices involved in the exercise of voice are at the center of much political sociology focused on the present: the study of public opinion, voting, volunteering, and social movement participation. But "voice" is also made possible by particular features of the broader social ordering and the organization of power.

From Political Order to "The Political"

One of the most influential political sociologists, Karl Marx, characterized history as the product of ongoing conflicts between economic groups organized through what are now described as processes of social closure: "The history of all hitherto existing society is the history of class struggles. Freeman and slave, patrician and plebeian, lord and serf, guild-master and journeyman, in a word, oppressor and oppressed, stood in constant opposition to one another" (Tucker 1978: 473–4). Restated in terms of social cages and social closure, varying forms of the economic division of labor have produced different configurations of dominant and subordinate groups, both mobilized through processes of social closure. In many cases, the result is direct conflict in the form of strikes and rebellions and even revolutions.

But on the way to modern society, a novel thing happened. Social spaces and practices devoted specifically to handling such conflicts developed. The right of subjects to petition a ruler might be acknowledged. In time, courts were established in which subjects could make claims on the basis of rights that were often newly recognized but expressed in a language of appeals to ancient principles. Some of the most enduringly influential of these innovations appeared in the ancient Mediterranean world, in the practices of Athenian democracy and the Roman Republic. Although property ownership or family lineage was almost always a condition for leadership, the selection and appointment of leaders (from among those who qualified) came to be governed by institutions such as lotteries or by consent on the part of some of the population (those who qualified). In these ways, control over political power was potentially partially disembedded from other social roles and networks.

In these political orders, a portion of the community took on a new status: citizen. The qualifications for citizenship were constituted out of multiple, often reinforcing, forms of social closure: adult, male, property-owning, and born into the community. Minors, women, slaves, the poor, foreigners – in various ways, any dependency or different-ness provided grounds for exclusion. But those who were accorded the rights of citizen within a particular community secured access to a new kind of social arena specifically designed for reflection upon the character of political order itself. Although built upon a complex map of social closures and within a social cage, these new institutions constituted "the political" as a domain of freedom to reflect upon the distribution and legitimacy of power.

The conception of "the political" as a zone of freedom has been an enduring source of confusion in the relationship between political theory and political sociology. The conceptual challenge for political sociology is to think about the relationship of networks of ties, embeddedness, dependence, and constraint to the specific institutional spheres constructed for deliberation over issues of public concern. When and why is the inequality and domination produced by social closure contested? And when is it accepted as inevitable or not even noticed? What are the social processes by which aspects of the social cages in which we live are brought into question, debated in the institutions that are designated as explicitly "political" and charged with (re)considering the organization of power? These questions often focus analysis on questions of structure and constraint rather than agency and freedom. Yet this confining analytic framework has been challenged by increasing attention to an element of modern political orders that appears particularly linked to possibilities for the exercise of voice and mobilizations that contest existing relations of power: civil society.

Linguistically, the concept of civil society is tied up with the Latin terms that also gave us words for city, citizenship, and civilian; these terms themselves were linked to the

Greek *polis* or city that gives us the root for political. Notice immediately the characteristic puzzle about these terms; they are all political in some sense, but none can be directly equated with the state or the durable organization of power. If one conceptualizes states as the tightest, most central components of a social cage, the adjective "civic" often described the adjoining domains, persons, and concerns.

In an influential formulation of this concept, Jürgen Habermas began by drawing on the philosopher Hannah Arendt in focusing on how the emergence of an economy based on private property produced a "private sphere of society that has become publicly relevant" (1994: 19). This definition centers on the historical differentiation of the economic as a realm separate from the household of the ruler, a process associated with the emergence of "modernity" and a recognizable *bourgeoisie* or middle class. This domain of exchange among private individuals, households, and firms could then be recognized as an object of "public," in the sense of "shared," concern. In Habermas' terms, "the bourgeois public sphere may be conceived above all as the sphere of private people come together as a public; they soon claimed the public sphere regulated from above against the public authorities themselves, to engage them in a debate over the general rules governing relations in the basically privatized but publicly relevant sphere of commodity exchange and social labor" (1994: 27). Through the emergence of a field of interaction constituted by debate over social and economic relations, in which arguments were won or lost on the basis of reason rather than deference to rulers, early modern Europe witnessed the establishment of a basis for exercising and contesting political rule, at least with respect to its regulation of the civil sphere (1994: 52). As Habermas concludes this piece of his argument: "*The fully developed bourgeois public sphere was based on the fictitious identity of the two roles assumed by the privatized individuals who came together to form a public: the role of property owners and the role of human beings pure and simple*" (1994: 56; original emphasis). In the conceptual imagination of those participating in these early modern civic debates, they become the fully realized, natural individuals who figured in the political theory of Rousseau, Locke, and others.

If the concept of a privately ordered but publicly relevant sphere began as an economic argument, it has led to theorizations of "civil society" that highlight a wide range of voluntary activity that are not oriented to trade and manufacture. Whether motivated by efforts to organize a profession, to create solidarities based on ethnicity or religion, to organize charity, or to enhance sociability, civic associations share a key feature with Habermas' understanding of the bourgeois public sphere: they are private realms in which actors reflect on and develop the skills to act on public issues and to reflect on the "public good." In this sense, civil society is a social domain outside of formal political institutions that often sustains the cultivation of a capacity to act politically and exercise voice.

Among the most famous claims made for the political significance of civil society is Alexis de Tocqueville's *Democracy in America* (2004). Visiting a still young United States from France in 1831, he sought to understand why one revolution in the name of equality had produced a relatively stable democracy, while the French Revolution had been followed by a sequence of regime shifts, including a period of dictatorship and a return to monarchy. A critical piece of the answer, he argued, was that the vibrant associational life he found in the United States kept the "spirit of liberty" alive and cultivated capacities for managing conflicts and producing public goods that did not require help from the state and, therefore, did not produce pressures for the expansion and centralization of state powers. In this way, associations may function as "schools for citizenship" in which individuals develop the skills, habits, networks, and resources capable of empowering them as political participants (2004: 595).

The fact of being "not-for-profit" or "nongovernmental," however, does not guarantee that an organization will promote such political empowerment or offer a platform for developing critical perspectives on public affairs and government actions. As Nina Eliasoph (1998) has documented through compelling ethnographic studies of activist, leisure, and volunteer organizations, the "etiquettes" that are expected by participants in such settings may sometimes discourage the development of capacities for voice. To understand the capacity of civil society to support political engagement and contestation, therefore, we need to attend to both the extent of social space beyond the control of direct governmental rule and the character of the organizations and associations that come to populate that space. Both factors generate the potential to contest political ordering from within the framework of a particular social cage.

What is Political Sociology?

Starting from Weber's definition of power, this chapter has constructed a basic conceptual vocabulary for thinking about the core question of political sociology: How can we explain the emergence, reproduction, and transformation of different forms of political ordering? In combination, the development of social cages, social closure, and restrictions on exit allow for the formation of durable systems of political hierarchy and the conditions for intensified extraction and coercion. As Tilly has argued, these processes may be amplified by war, but they may also be moderated (or exacerbated) by actions within new institutional arenas that are explicitly devoted to deliberations over political order. In some settings, the grievances generated by exploitation and coercion may fail to produce political mobilization as Gaventa observed in Appalachia. But in other cases, petitions, demonstrations, elections, and deliberations function as methods for reconstructing political orders in ways that make continued social co-existence and cooperation possible.

This last point, however, may strike some as hopelessly old-fashioned. In an era of widespread conflict and entrenched policy challenges, there is ample evidence of the limited ability of political institutions to resolve social problems. Legislatures are gridlocked, electorates volatile, and executive power too often appears impotent in the face of major challenges. But the constitutional design of formal institutions does not exhaust the many ways in which politics happens in modern societies. Political sociology explores both how social processes shape outcomes within formal political institutions and the many kinds of politics that play out in settings outside of recognized governing arrangements. These include the intimate politics of the family as well as the civic associations and social networks that sustain social movements and political campaigns that cross the boundary back into the domain of formal political institutions. So to understand the character of political institutions and how – or how well – they work, we also need to understand how formal political institutions are embedded in this expansive, sociological sense of politics.

2
States, Empires, Nation-States

The opening archeological tour of castles and temples and civic monuments in chapter 1 reminded us that the organization of power has taken a great many forms. That variety, in turn, poses questions for political sociology. If small-scale systems of durable power develop in such diverse ways, how and why did they eventually produce the large-scale systems of political order that structure the modern world? Who came to be incorporated in these political orders and in what ways? And, finally, how have these expansive systems of political organization interacted with one another, producing what we have now come to know as geopolitics and increasingly global economies?

"States," in very general terms, can be described as a central set of institutions from which political relations – including authoritative rule-making and control of political violence – extend to cover a territory (Mann 1986: 37). But the arrangement of those political relations can take different forms. Surveying the past few centuries, two different ways of constructing a state have been particularly prominent: empires and nation-states. The key differences between these distinct solutions to the puzzle of how to construct a state can be captured by the relationship between the character of rule (direct or indirect) and its relationship to group membership or identity. Empires rest on extensive relations of indirect rule without a corresponding sense of shared cultural and political membership. "The central state negotiates and maintains more or less distinct compacts between itself and the various segments of this polity" and, as a consequence, "most of the different segments of the polity remain largely unconnected among themselves" resulting in a "hub-and-spoke network structure, where the rim is absent" (Barkey 2008: 9). Thus the Roman Empire encompassed provinces stretching from Mesopotamia to Britain, all linked through the capital city and its official representatives, but not directly to one another.

In contrast to this hub-and-spoke imagery, nation-states are closer to what we imagine when looking at a modern map of the world: territorially bounded entities that join a cultural framework of membership – the nation or the people – directly to a system of organized rule. As we will see, this way of thinking about the coincidence of membership, social relations, and political organization is itself the product of the historical emergence of nationalism and the nation-state. It suggests that those contained within national borders share important similarities such as language, cuisine, and even reproductive practices (Watkins 1991; Weber 1978 [1918–20]: 395–8). At the borders between such nation-states, languages change, laws change, money changes, and wars develop. The administration of these differences is a central activity of the government encircled by those boundaries. State officials issue passports, print stamps, and regulate a school curriculum that instills a proper sense of national identity and patriotic fervor in the members of each new generation born within those borders (Brubaker 1996).

Both nation-states and empires figure prominently in the development of the contemporary political world. A subset of states, the European powers, extended their reach around the globe through a succession of empires: Portuguese, Spanish, Dutch, British, French, and German. Both Russia and China expanded territorially across Asia in processes of imperial expansion followed by more or less complete incorporation in national configurations. Centered in Istanbul, the Ottoman Empire at its peak encompassed large portions of both Europe and Asia. The Americas were colonized and subdivided by multiple imperial powers – Portuguese, Spanish, French, British and, along a sliver of the Pacific Coast, Russian.

The coastlines of Africa were dotted by strongholds of trading empires and, in the nineteenth century, the interior of the continent – or at least its maps – was reorganized by a competitive rush of imperial powers to claim colonial rights over territory. Japan followed a similar model, extending its control through parts of the Western Pacific while, by the late nineteenth century, an ascendant United States would build its own empire in the Pacific and the Caribbean. In all their different forms, these political systems were based on imperialism as a system of indirect rule, "a strategy of political control over foreign lands that does not necessarily involve conquest, occupation, and durable rule by outside invaders" (Steinmetz 2014: 79).

These patterns of conquest and settlement set in train further conflicts and transformations. In North America, conflicts over the "rights" of colonists as Englishmen fueled what would become the first revolution for national independence, quickly followed by the Haitian Revolution (1791–1895) which undercut France's key foothold in the slave economies of the Caribbean and its forward base in terms of expansion into the Americas. Over the course of the nineteenth century, other Portuguese and Spanish colonies in Latin America made successful claims for their independence, declaring themselves to be republics. In each of these cases, the claims for autonomy as a state were linked to claims of membership in a nation, a people entitled to self-government. Empires continued to generate conflicts for national independence around the globe, culminating in a wave of decolonization in the years between the end of the Second World War and 1960 that produced a planet organized in the increasingly standardized form of the nation-state (Meyer et al. 1997; Strang 1992).

These episodes of imperial extension, consolidation of state power, and claims for national independence can be approached with a basic set of analytic tools: differences between direct and indirect rule as well as variations in the character of political membership, particularly that powerful form that we know as nationalism. Out of these basic building blocks, actors in very different settings have constructed durable, expansive, intensive, and consequential systems for organizing and exerting power.

Direct and Indirect Rule

Organized rule appears in settings that Michael Mann described as "social cages": "the containment of human beings behind clear, fixed, confined social and territorial boundaries" (1986: 38). As recognizable "states" emerge through the exercise of central control over local systems of inequality and cooperation, a persistent kind of competition develops. In attempting to extend the scope and scale of central power, those in control enter into competition with their counterparts in more local systems of ranked social organization. The would-be ruler advances his (almost always his rather than hers) project of rule by exerting power over local notables and village leaders. But in exerting that control, the would-be ruler can take two importantly different strategic approaches.

The first approach is one of "indirect rule" that seeks "to co-opt local and regional powerholders without utterly transforming their bases of power." At any given time, a would-be ruler may have built central institutions of power that control a limited territory, but "beyond that scale ... they had no choice but to bargain with the authorities of competing centers" (Tilly 1992: 24–5). In some cases, one center may come to dominate but exert its authority indirectly through the former ruler of another center who has now become a subordinate authority. Under conditions of indirect rule, the ascendant authority does not establish direct relations with the subjects of the subordinated authority. Instead, the persons or families who may once have been rulers in their own right, now function as local officials in a more extensive political configuration. These systems rest on bargains between the central ruler and those now-local notables: "All these arrangements left considerable power and discretion in the hands of local potentates, just so long as they contained the monarch's enemies and kept the revenues flowing to the national capital....indirect rule made it possible to govern without erecting, financing, and feeding a bulky administrative apparatus" (Tilly 1992: 25).

Systems of indirect rule involve a trade-off between lower administrative requirements on the center and a lack of control over and visibility into conditions in each locality. By depending on a local notable to collect taxes, for example, the central rulers are relieved of the cost of building an extensive apparatus for tax collection. But they then depend on local notables to provide honest accounts and to deliver the expected tax revenues at the appointed time. As a consequence, central rulers may seek to strengthen their control, either by adding new lines of officials to oversee local notables or inserting close allies into local systems of political order.

Julia Adams (1996) provides one example of this strategy – and its limits – in her study of the networks of governance in the Dutch Empire of the 1700s. In the territorially tiny "metropole" – the seat of central governing power – close relations and committee structures joined the elite families from different cities in the Netherlands. But the management of their vast trading empire, organized through the Dutch East Indies Company, required methods for exercising control over trade and revenue generated half way around the world, most importantly from Batavia (now Jakarta) in present-day Indonesia. The solution was to send sons, cousins, and nephews as representatives of the coalition of families that dominated the metropole. But those sons, cousins, and nephews were men, inclined to do what men will do. So other families formed in Batavia, based in alliances of these Dutch company men with the daughters of important lineages on the island of Java and beyond. And, as a consequence, loyalties were divided, between ties to a man's Dutch family and connections to the family of his partner and provision for their children together.

Given the limits of early modern transportation and communication technologies, there were few alternatives to some form of indirect rule. Even in what would eventually become centralized nation-states, earlier rulers depended upon the systems of exchange and loyalty with local elites that characterized the feudalism of the Middle Ages. Kings gave lords title to land and the associated population; lords reciprocated with military forces and tax revenues. The same form of relationship could then be repeated between lords and minor lords, then between minor lords and gentry. Any effort to extend direct rule from the center, whether in empires or proto-nation-states, required renegotiation of alliances: between central rulers and local notables; between local notables and peasants in peripheral regions; and, conceivably, between central rulers and urban residents. These rearrangements took place in multiple ways, advanced by building ties through intensified exchanges, by elaborating shared identities that reinforce new alignments, and by asserting – sometimes violently – new theories of legitimate authority (Kiser and Linton 2002; Kroneberg and Wimmer 2012: 188). Depending on the strategies pursued by different actors, these rearrangements produced many different kinds of regimes: monarchies (absolutist or constitutional), theocracies, republics, to name only a few. The basic dynamics, however, are rooted in the processes of social caging and closure discussed in the previous chapter: "These systems result from a struggle between actors endowed with different resources and unequal power who seek to enter into an exchange relationship with some actors while excluding others from their alliance system" (Kroneberg and Wimmer 2012: 177). How precisely this happens can be illustrated by a comparison of the architecture of political networks and shared identities in the Ottoman and Spanish Empires.

Culture and the Consolidation of Power: Tolerance and Nationalism

In a compelling study of the Ottoman Empire, Karen Barkey characterizes those who constructed the empire as formidable builders of networks within and across the ethnic, religious, and political identities that proliferated in the borderlands between a collapsing Roman Empire and the Safavid Empire centered in modern-day Iran (Barkey 2008). Centered at the northeast corner of the Mediterranean, this terrain was home to Jews, Christians (both Orthodox and "Latin"), Muslims (Sunni, Shi'ite, and Sufi), and a great many other ethnoreligious communities. As they organized for conflict, managed trade, and sought to consolidate control, Muslims married Christians (some of whom had converted), consulted with sages of many persuasions, respected mystics, and forged ties of comradeship that cross-cut other potential bases of loyalty. This same practice of networking across difference shaped a pattern of rule by many of those who emerged as dominant. The empire was understood to be stronger because of its diversity and so long as a fundamental subordination to Islam was recognized, communities and peripheral regions would be left to govern themselves to a considerable degree.

Although tolerance for diversity constituted one recipe for constructing an empire, this solution might be strained by the need of rulers to insure the loyalty of those who served them and the solidarity of those over whom they ruled. Recall how the Dutch Empire had relied on family ties – along with rotation of postings between metropole and imperial outposts – to hold the system together. But the trust based on interpersonal ties and shared loyalties in the metropole was threatened as empires grew in scale and scope. In the case of the Spanish Empire, which extended from Europe to the Americas and beyond, this "solution" to the organization of indirect rule gave way to something new, a rift in networks of kinship and economic ties based on the location of one's birth. Infant sons who traveled to the New World faced one set of opportunities in the imperial administration; their brothers born in the colonies faced a much more restricted set. It remained to the *creoles*, those born on the far side of that rift, to make new cultural sense of their situation. The result was a new cultural concept: nationalism. But, in a system of European states, many of which had built globe-spanning empires, "why was it precisely *creole* communities that developed so early conceptions of their nation-ness – *well before most of Europe?*" (Anderson 1991: 50).

The anthropologist Benedict Anderson traced the origins of nationalism to just such a rift in the social networks that bound empires together. Reflecting on the emergence of proto-national solidarities in the Spanish colonies of the Americas, Anderson takes the perspective of a talented and ambitious "creole," born outside the Kingdom of Spain: "Even if he was born within one week of his father's migration, the accident of birth in the Americas consigned him to subordination – even though in terms of language, religion, ancestry, or manners he was largely indistinguishable from the Spain-born Spaniard ... how irrational his exclusion must have seemed!" (1991: 57–8). These assumptions about who could – and could not – be promoted to the highest offices in empire and church created new boundaries of social closure through exclusion. That talented, ambitious creole would find that "the apex of his looping climb, the highest administrative centre to which he could be assigned, was the capital of the imperial administrative unit in which he found himself": Mexico City in Mexico, Santiago in Chile. "Yet on this cramped pilgrimage he found travelling-companions, who came to sense that their fellowship was based ... on the shared fatality of trans-Atlantic birth" (1991: 57).

In contrast to the indigenous people conquered through the force of European armaments and the temptations of trade (aided by new germs and the epidemics that followed, see Diamond 1997), the *creoles* "had virtually the same relationship to arms, disease, Christianity and European culture as the metropolitans. In other words, in principle, they had readily at hand the political, cultural and military means for successfully asserting themselves" (Anderson 1991: 58). In such a situation, peripheral elites and peripheral masses (Kroneberg and Wimmer 2012) could unite in an effort to unravel the ties of indirect rule that kept them within the structure of imperial rule.

A similar dynamic played out in the English colonies of North America in the late eighteenth century. Understanding themselves as Englishmen with the rights of Englishmen, many of the colonists were dismayed when the Parliament in London began to impose new taxes in an effort to right the imperial finances strained by years of conflict in what Americans would come to call the "French-Indian Wars" (themselves one of many arenas of what Europeans would know as the Seven Years War). The rallying cry of "no taxation without representation" captures a sense of exclusion similar to that felt by the Spanish creoles whose careers within the empire were constrained by the location of their birth. Yet, to the extent that their political identities were as "Englishmen and Virginians" or "Englishmen and New Yorkers," cultural work had to be done to create a shared identity that could anchor the establishment of a new nation-state. This effort built on experiences of collaboration and coalition, a process of recognizing the residents of other colonies as compatriots who were worthy of loyalty and sacrifice: "Trust-building involved more than strategic consideration. As ordinary Americans affirmed their trust-worthiness through revolutionary acts that were then quickly reported in the popular press, they discovered the language of rights and liberty was more than rhetoric. Within a framework of local groups that came to identify with similar groups in distant places, people translated personal sacrifice into revolutionary ideology" (Breen 2004: xiii). As Weber argued of race and ethnicity (1978 [1918–20]: 385–98), political conflict produced new collective identities out of equivalent positions within a structure of imperial rule.

Cultures of nationalism developed first on the peripheries of empires, but the political project of building a "people" then traveled back to the political centers or metropoles where rulers faced new challenges of legitimacy, generated in part by the emergence of what Habermas described as the "bourgeois public sphere" (chapter 1). This new domain of public discourse, centered on shared concerns for an economic system built on private property, energized novel forms of political mobilization. In turn, new patterns of political mobilization triggered experimentation with new mechanisms of political control and new bases for political identity.

The Construction of the Modern Nation-State

The emergence of the nation-state as a dominant form of political order can be traced through a number of the first global empires. Benedict Anderson's investigation into the origins of nationalism followed a path through the Spanish Empire, but comparable sequences were unfolding elsewhere. Anchored in a marshy region at the northwestern corner of Europe, the Dutch Empire had its origins as a province within yet another empire, that of Hapsburg Spain. Differentiated in many ways from those in central power, and above all by the divides created by the Protestant Reformation, the urban "bourgeoisie" – merchants and other property owners

– united in a conflict to throw off Spanish rule. Once they succeeded, after years of bloody battles, these new political elites faced another challenge: how to gain the consent and obedience of those over whom they sought to rule.

The outcome, evident in many places beyond the Netherlands, was a new way of ordering political power. This shift, argued the French philosopher Michel Foucault (1926–84), could be understood in terms of the emergence of new modes of governing, from those that focused on the management of things and property to the management of populations. Foucault termed this new kind of management "biopolitics" (Foucault 2010). As state administrative structures developed, they were elaborated and sustained by the emergence of new kinds of trained personnel and practices that allowed states to collect taxes based on property and trade (Brewer 1988). The change can be seen in the differences between a modern census and the great Domesday Book of 1086 in which William the Conqueror of England sought to have the ownership of lands, livestock, and property catalogued throughout his new realm. The modern census, invented during the same eras that saw the beginnings of mass schooling and early social policies, takes the population itself as the central resource of the sovereign. So in addition to counting acres, cattle, sheep, and hides, a modern census documents the attributes of persons who might be useful to the state: age, gender, race, sometimes religion, sometimes education and occupation. To move from counting to managing these populations, however, required new political techniques.

The need to manage the population itself was clear to the local Dutch elites who gained control as a result of their successful rebellion against the Hapsburg Empire. To this end, these empowered Protestants invented new ways of harnessing religious belief to the maintenance of political order, thereby producing legitimacy and loyalty along with constraint. They created novel institutions, including a "house of discipline" established in 1596. This was, in effect, a machine for producing compliance with expected behavior within the division of labor that was the new Dutch Republic: "Through a strict regimen of social isolation, forced labor, corporal punishment, and moral instruction, able-bodied beggars ... were taught the value of work and transformed into productive citizens" (Gorski 2003: 63). One foreign observer set down a description of "a drowning cell" in which an inmate would be locked; the room would then be steadily flooded with water until "finally up to his neck when he found that he had been cured of his idleness and, fearing that he would drown, began ... furious pumping until he had emptied the room, when he discovered that his weaknesses had left him and he had to confess his cure" (Gorski 2003: 65). Although, as one eminent historian notes, the tale may be a "bizarre fable, a sadistic fantasy" (Schama 1988: 23), the image of the drowning cell serves as a metaphor for the coercive production of a new kind of self, an internalization of the behavioral norms and identities required to stabilize a system of rule. As Philip Gorski explains, the Dutch Republic illustrates how an ascetic religion such as Calvinism produces "an ethic of self-discipline within individual believers," inspires the invention of "institutional strategies for maintaining collective discipline within the church," and generates arguments for broader social reforms that promote discipline. The result, Gorski argues, was not only a new kind of state – a powerful social cage – but a new kind of modern self or political subject.

Other regimes turned to different cultural strategies in pursuit of a stable political order. In medieval Japan, central rulers were concerned not only with the obedience of the disadvantaged but also the loyalty and control of the samurai warriors who had played a central role in securing the domination of the emperor – and the shadow rule of the shogun – over the entire territory of what we now know as modern Japan. At the heart of this process is a cultural puzzle: how is the "so-called collective and harmonious culture in Japan ... paradoxically connected with a history of conflicts and struggles." Just as nation-building in North America involved the development of trust and identification among residents of separate colonies, and the consolidation of the Dutch Republic occurred through the disciplining of the population through religiously-infused practices, the cementing of centralized rule in Japan entailed transformations in the cultural selves of those with the most potential to disrupt the new system of rule. As Eiko Ikegami explains, "from its inception, the military culture of the samurai included an emphasis on discipline, with the expectation that honorable warriors would control their short-term desires in order to achieve long-term goals." State-building involved channeling "this tradition of self-discipline to produce a mental disposition conducive to harmonizing each individual's sense of personal identity with accepted social goals and responsibilities" (1995: 11).

Whether the problems of loyalty, discipline, and control were confronted by urban merchants in the Dutch Republic or the Japanese shogun, leaders faced a similar set of choices about how to organize rule. These decisions often turned on the particular mix of different dimensions of power as presented by Gaventa: power exerted directly against another's will as in Weber's classic definition, operating through differential access to agendas or decisions, or working through the naturalization of inequalities such that possible grievances are not even formulated. As the Italian philosopher Antonio Gramsci (1971: 57–8) famously argued, rule may take the form of "domination" (direct force) or "hegemony" which operates through the power of a culture of taken-for-grantedness. Domination – which is akin to Weber's basic sense of carrying out one's will "despite resistance" from another – is a resource-intensive method of rule. It requires mobilizing force and rewarding allies, as well as anticipating resistance from those who are dominated. If the resistance is sufficiently strong, subordinated groups may be able to demand new rights and policies in exchange for the creation of new state powers. Consequently, the incentives to find alternatives to domination increase as state leaders attempt to extend and intensify systems of direct rule.

The history of efforts to extend and strengthen systems of direct rule is marked by the invention of new techniques for mapping, counting, and penetrating the economic and social lives of their subjects. These methods "gave rulers access to citizens and the resources they controlled through household taxation, mass conscription, censuses, police systems, and many other invasions of small-scale social life. But it did so at the cost of widespread resistance, extensive bargaining, and the creation of rights and perquisites for citizens. Both the penetration and the bargaining laid down new state structures, inflating the government's budgets, personnel, and organizational diagrams. The omnivorous state of our own time took shape" (Tilly 1992: 25). But the appetites of those seeking greater revenues for the state and control for its leaders were always at risk from resistance, and even rebellion, from those on the receiving end of extraction and domination (chapter 3). These efforts to enhance the powers of centralized states were also endangered by commercial and military projects that extended beyond their own boundaries.

Shaped by War, Trade, and Liberation

In discussing the history of domestic efforts to extend and intensify control within centralized administrations, it is easy to assume that there have always been tightly organized states that can be treated, in a sort of analytic shorthand, as singular actors with singular purposes. But the effort of building any kind of state, whether empire or nation-state, always involves multiple projects including the management of domestic populations and of foreign relations, both economic and military (Foucault 2010: 5). The result may take the form of factional politics within the central state or produce mutually reinforcing cycles, in which improved methods of tax collection enable support of more powerful armies or navies (Brewer 1988). Charles Tilly (1992: 70–1) highlights the intersecting roles of war and policing: "Europeans followed a standard war-provoking logic: everyone who controlled substantial coercive means tried to maintain a secure area within which he could enjoy the returns from coercion, plus a fortified buffer zone, possibly run at a loss, to protect the secure area. Police or their equivalent deployed force in the secure area, while armies patrolled the buffer zone and ventured outside it."

With a secure interior and controlled boundaries, states can set other dynamics in motion, notably the expansion of trade organized through imperial relations or global markets.

As John Darwin writes, the prominent place of Britain in the world "was not simply a consequence of Britain's 'own' power and its ability to impose it wholesale on the rest of the globe. Instead, the key to British power lay in combining the strength of its overseas components with that of the imperial centre, and managing them – not commanding them – through the various linkages of 'imperial politics': some persuasive, some coercive, some official, some unofficial" (2009: 13). Just as the potency of social cages is grounded in a combination of interdependence, loyalty, and lack of opportunity for exit, the same kinds of dynamics are replicated at regional and global scales in the consolidation of imperial systems which may extend beyond the formal boundaries of empire and the span of even somewhat direct control on the part of imperial officials.

One of the forces holding together these complex systems of empire was the sense of at least some of those incorporated into systems of indirect rule that the benefits of taking a subordinate role in an imperial regime outweighed the costs. Benefits might take the form of participation in systems of trade, access to more powerful medical technologies, the promise of salvation from religious missionaries, or opportunities for formal education both in new colonial schools and, for a few, in the colleges and universities of the metropole. But these calculations were, of course, always subject to revision and contestation. And recalculations of the cost–benefit outcomes could be prompted by developments in the central states of an empire as well as by grievances at the periphery.

Many of these changes were key elements of the emergence of the modern nation-state: the linking of administrative power to a cultural sense of membership or nationhood; the increased capacity for war-making; and, to anticipate the chapter to come, the linking of national belonging to principles of popular sovereignty, even in very limited forms. The first of these changes blocked an earlier understanding of the relationship of imperial center to provinces that was based on principles and practices of toleration and appreciation of diversity (Barkey 2008: 13). As Barkey demonstrates, even the Ottoman Empire eventually turned from the embrace of diversity under the pressure of military competition from the Russian and Hapsburg Empires (as well as economic competition from Europe), as leaders increasingly invoked forms of "nationalism" to sustain military mobilization.

The growing cultural power of nationalism drove other changes in the relationship between metropolitan powers and their far-flung settlements. If "nationalism" had been invented as a response to the "fatality of trans-Atlantic birth" and as a way of understanding an abyss that opened up between the life chances of genetically and culturally similar Spanish-born Spaniards and *creoles* (Anderson 1991), it operated in a still harsher way to structure relationships between imperial powers and provinces in the face of significant differences in physical appearance and cultural practice. The system of indirect rule that is central to empire as a political form can be compared to a narrower meaning of colonialism: "the conquest of a foreign people followed by the creation of an organization controlled by members of the conquering polity and suited to rule over the conquered territory's indigenous population" (Steinmetz 2014: 79).

Whereas local rulers were key nodes in an extended network of rule and exchange, colonialism was based on an understanding of colonizer and colonized as different and unequal (in terms of legal standing, social or civilizational status, racial or biological difference, religion, and so forth). The result was an often brutal collision of practices of domination and cultural standards that generated harsh new cultural models. Writing of forced labor in the colonies, which was based on intimidation and visible oppression rather than contract, the philosopher Jean-Paul Sartre (1905–80) described how this led French soldiers to reject "metropolitan universalism": "since none can rob, enslave, or kill his fellow man without committing a crime, they lay down the principle that the colonized subject is not a fellow man ... Colonial violence not only aims at keeping the enslaved men at a respectful distance, it also seeks to dehumanize them" (Sartre 2004 [1961]: xlix–l). This intensification of the "othering" of the colonized, an extreme form of social closure, is the flip side of the creation of those common categories of membership central to nationalism.

The emphasis placed on cultural and physical difference in these later stages of empire, however, opened up new political possibilities. In an imperial province or colony, local elites and masses would find themselves on the same side of that fateful divide. No matter how "civilized" and educated and fluent in the language of the metropole, one born to parents of local descent would be marked as "not belonging" to the civilizational and political center of empire. In such a situation, local elites might shift alliances, trading loyalty to metropolitan elites for solidarity with colonial masses (Kroneberg and Wimmer 2012: 180). Such shifts were often linked to the resentment of exclusion from increasingly nationalist – and by extension racial – forms of social closure in the metropole. The writings of the political theorist Frantz Fanon (1925–61) trace the psychopolitical damage inflicted on the colonized in the French holdings in both the Caribbean and North Africa. "The violence of the colonized," he argues, "unifies the people. By its very structure colonialism is separatist and regionalist. Colonialism is not merely content to note the existence of tribes, it reinforces and differentiates them." In Fanon's analysis, this sharpening of the boundaries of identity through the practices of colonial rule is then intensified by popular mobilization in the struggle for liberation which "introduces the notion of common cause, national destiny, and collective history into every consciousness. Consequently, the second phase, i.e., nation building, is facilitated by the existence of this mortar kneaded with blood and rage" (2004 [1961]: 51).

Such anger could combine with political aspirations to the popular sovereignty already achieved in many of those nation-states that were at the center of empires. As middle- and eventually working-class men in Britain and France gained the right to vote – whether through decades of protest or repeated revolutions (chapter 3) – the absence of principles of self-government in the colonies generated deep grievances: "Where the metropolitan model is grounded in popular sovereignty, nationalism, and a broadly incorporative state, it is a weapon easily turned against its creators ... Its universalism and communisms make the nation-state a powerful model for peripheral political mobilization" (Strang 1990: 847). David Strang demonstrates the power of this model through an "event-history" analysis of decolonization, in which the unit of analysis is country-year and the outcome of interest is the transition from non-independence to independence. Strang finds strong effects of the extent of popular sovereignty in the nation-state at the center of an empire on that empire's colony: "Broad metropolitan suffrage regimes substantially raise the rate of decolonization in the metropole's dependency. The addition of a third of the population to the metropolitan electorate (a typical increment when universal male suffrage is achieved, or when universal suffrage replaces universal male suffrage) quintuples the estimated rate" (Strang 1990: 854). So when the vote is extended to all adult men in Britain, the probability that British colonies will gain independence increases and, then, increases again when British women gain the vote. In this way, powerful cultural assumptions about citizenship flow along the ideological networks formed within imperial systems.

Given this relationship between the political models in force in the central (or metropolitan) state of an empire and the politics put in motion in its colonies, the practice of "empire" turns out to be particularly challenging for nation-states founded on principles of equality and universalism. One response is the rejection of "metropolitan universalism" that Sartre described at work in the systems of forced labor in France's north African colonies. By contrast, according to Julian Go, proponents of "American empire" have asserted a model grounded in claims of "democratic tutelage" in which "The United States would be an empire, but unlike other empires it would use its power benevolently, taking up the task of transforming, uplifting, and democratizing foreign peoples" (2007: 76, 79). Commentators from other imperial traditions made note of the strangeness of this effort in terms that were often condescending. In the words of the wife of a British diplomat writing in her diary in 1906:

> The [American] Ideal is this you see, that every people in the world should have self-government and equal rights. This means ... that they consider these Malay half-breeds to be capable ... of understanding the motives, and profiting by the institutions which it has taken the highest white races two or three thousand years to evolve. [...] When I come to think of

it, America with this funny little possession of hers is like a mother with her first child, who ... tries to bring it up on some fad of her own because it is so much more precious and more wonderful than any other child any one else ever had. (Quoted in Go 2007: 82)

As the United States began to develop its imperial system – against the criticism of those who were sure that "empire" would destroy the nation's republican system of government – Americans did adopt a model that differed from other imperial traditions while often falling dramatically short of the proclaimed ideal of "democratic tutelage." Assumptions about the "civilizational" level or potential of the inhabitants of different colonies and protectorates led to the founding of schools and a version of civilian government in the Philippines and Puerto Rico, while very few schools were established by the naval governors of Samoa and Guam. But, as those supporting independence for the Philippines would learn, when the terms of "democratic tutelage" were rejected in the name of popular sovereignty, repression could be swift and harsh (see chapter 3).

Precisely because the systems of political order and membership *within* the metropolitan nation-state often differed from those *between* the metropolitan nation-state and its colonies, both military and ideological force had to be marshaled to maintain the networks that constituted the imperial system. In Tilly's vocabulary, the terms of social closure and membership in the nation-state at the core of empire generated tension throughout empire. Those tensions, in turn, have generated war and trade and still more war, shaping the political landscape of our present and the future still in formation.

Politics and the Paths of Social Change

These projects of building empires and nation-states are easily relegated to historical analysis and understood as part of the prehistory of modern politics. Yet the revival of a language of "American Empire" at the end of the twentieth century should remind us that the advantages and disadvantages of different forms of political order shift with time and the calculations of a changing cast of political actors. At the beginning of this century, highly placed advisers in Washington DC were quoted as urging Americans to "re-conceive their global power from one of a traditional nation-state to an imperial power." It was time to recognize that "we're an empire now, and when we act, we create our own reality" (quoted in Go 2007: 74–5). In the wake of the terrorist attacks on New York and Washington DC on September 11, 2001, these same advisers would confront the challenges of meeting a non-state, non-territorial, but strategically focused opponent in a new form of global conflict. As they learned all too well, nothing is inevitable about the delimited, democratic nation-state as a form of political order.

By highlighting the dynamics set in motion by the mix of indirect rule, direct rule, and membership, it is not hard to see how these processes play out in contemporary politics beyond the outlines of the "global war on terror." In the fall of 2014, for example, Scotland voted on a proposal for independence from the United Kingdom (it failed, but was followed less than a year later by an almost complete electoral sweep of parliamentary seats by the Scottish National Party), Hong Kong was roiled by protests against the announced arrangement by which the government in Beijing would have the power to approve those eligible to run in upcoming elections. In Spain, proponents of independence for the region of Catalonia spent these same months agitating for an independence vote and, eventually, organizing an election without authorization from the government in Madrid. In each of these cases, contemporary politics activates cleavages that were not completely erased by earlier processes of moving from indirect to direct rule, reinforced by the construction of an overarching sense of national belonging.

But the cases of Scotland, Hong Kong, and Catalonia have something else in common, namely an apparatus of popular elections as a framework for political legitimacy. Although partial and threatened in the case of Hong Kong, this way of organizing politics around the principle of popular sovereignty has fueled the aspirational politics of national liberation in many of the colonial struggles for independence discussed in this chapter. But that model itself was the produce of other struggles, often largely internal to established political orders, although sometimes catalyzed by pressures of war or economic competition. In order to trace the genealogy of democratic models, the next chapter turns to the political sociology of revolution and the paths taken to a variety of modern regimes.

3
Regimes and Revolutions

Viewed on a global scale, across centuries and even millennia, the world's political landscapes pulse and shift forms. Local orders – grounded in the exercise of military power or control of sacred places or advantageous locations for trade – extend their influence through arrangements of indirect rule. Over time, these relations may intensify and become linked to cultural categories of membership and solidarity, resulting in nation-states. At other times, in other places, networks of indirect rule extend outwards, controlling but not incorporating new territory and community, producing varieties of empire. But, whatever the arrangement of political power in any given place on any given day, those arrangements shape the politics that follow.

As we shall see in later chapters on democratic politics (chapters 4 and 5), the organization of power often generates politics that create strong positive feedback effects, reinforcing existing institutions, practices, and distributions of resources. But before we turn to make sense of democratic politics, we need to understand the historical emergence of democratic regimes. How, after thousands of years of monarchies, theocracies, empires, and countless other orderings of political power, did it happen that principles of "one person, one vote" and "free and fair elections" would be taken as standards for – if not accurate descriptions of – what political life should be?

The social theorists who helped to establish the discipline of sociology provide a starting point for answering this question. In the work of thinkers such as Auguste Comte (1798–1857), Emile Durkheim (1858–1917), or Karl Marx (1818–83), history is understood either as a sequence of types of social organization or as movement along a continuum from one type of social organization to another. These types were not purely political, but characterized in terms of the division of labor and different forms of authority (Clemens 2005: 495–9). For Comte, history appeared as a sequence of types distinguished by different forms of authority: theological, metaphysical, and scientific. For Durkheim, history was imagined as movement along a continuum defined by differentiation generated by the division of labor, from *mechanical solidarity* to *organic solidarity*. This transition between forms of authority is accompanied by a shift in the character of law (and by extension other forms of state action) that move from punishment toward restitution and rehabilitation. With Marx, both shifts in the bases of authority and the organization of economic activity are joined in an imagery of history as "the history of class struggles" (Tucker 1978: 473–4).

These imageries of historical change pose three large questions for political sociology. First, how can we characterize social change in political terms? Second, what are the political processes that drive social change and how are they generated? Finally, given the emergence of forces sufficient to reordering political life, how can we understand what determines the shape and character of the political orders that are reassembled or invented? Restated in terms of our basic theoretical toolkit, when do processes of social closure generate mobilizations with the potential to reorder the organization of rule, and how is the taken-for-grantedness of that rule undermined? These puzzles form much of the subject matter of the sociology of political change, revolution, and regime formation.

Combination and Sequence

For sociologists working in the decades after the Second World War, questions about trajectories of political change were neither abstract nor academic. Informed by the experience of mass war against Nazi Germany, in uneasy alliance with Soviet Russia, these scholars often posed the question of political change in terms that captured the stakes in the Cold War. Barrington Moore captured the essence of this puzzle in the title of his classic *Social Origins of Dictatorship and Democracy* (1966) and provided the outlines of an answer in the subtitle, *Lord and Peasant in the Making of the Modern World*. Exemplifying what has come to be described as a "structuralist" approach to the study of political change, Moore identified class power – and specifically the pattern of alliances among economic classes – as the key factor determining which path to modernity would be followed in a given country.

Moore's framing of the question exemplifies one important difference from the imageries of history found in Comte, Durkheim, and Marx. Rather than explaining a single trajectory of change, Moore was interested in the divergence of distinct paths and multiple outcomes. His argument parted from Marxian explanations of modernity on another key point. Rather than focusing on the rise of capitalism understood as industrialism and, therefore, on the relations of exploitation between employer and employee, Moore argued that the key determinants of the path of political change lay in the countryside: "The ways in which the landed upper classes and the peasants reacted to the challenge of commercial agriculture were decisive factors in determining the political outcome" (1966: xvii). In different combinations, landed elites and peasants might ally with or against commercial elites, with or against a growing population of urban workers, a dynamic that echoes the shifting alliances among peripheral elites and masses in research on empires (chapter 2; Kroneberg and Wimmer 2012) as well as in the uneven capacity of elites to control the trajectory of change (Lachmann 1990). These varying responses to the advance of commercial agriculture, Moore argues, tipped the balance between the "bourgeois" path to democracy (when landed elites allied with others to embrace capitalism), the fascist path (when landed and commercial elites allied to suppress workers and peasants alike), or the totalitarian path in which thorough-going peasant revolution swept aside traditional elites and created the conditions for establishing a new kind of strong, centralized state.

Presented schematically, Moore's argument focuses on specific classes and is fundamentally combinatorial. Yet as he developed each case within his comparative study, an additional dimension of analysis emerged. These shifting alliances among classes are formed in political cultures that carry durable orientations toward the legitimacy of different configurations of power. Thus the patterns of alliance that produced the "bourgeois" path to capitalist democracy in England and Western Europe were formed in a historical context favorable to limitations on the power of the state. In Moore's argument, the legacies of feudalism (see chapter 2) included "the growth of the notion of the immunity of certain groups and persons from the power of the ruler, along with the conception of the right of resistance to unjust authority" (1966: 415). This line of argument has been refined through careful comparison of the variations in land-holding regimes in different parts of England and their consequences for different trajectories of political development (Somers 1993). More recent scholarship on the political development of Western Europe has strengthened the case for the lasting influence of Roman law and medieval parliaments in shaping the extent of political liberties and monarchical power in early modern states (Downing 1992; Ertman 1997).

This attention to legacies and institutional context underscores the importance of time and sequence in shaping trajectories of political change. With respect to the development of democratic politics, scholars have paid particular attention to the order of appearance of rational bureaucracy. For this line of research, the comparison between the United States and Britain has been particularly important. Reflecting a Cold War set of preferences about political outcomes, scholars sought to understand why the United States had established a relatively robust system of party competition, but one that had been plagued by problems of patronage politics (often seen as a threat to newly independent nations in the decades after the Second World War), while Britain was characterized by a much more professionalized administrative state but a slower, more incremental, expansion of the right to vote, even among men. Reinhard Bendix (1964) attributed these outcomes to the same dynamics of elite and class alliance now familiar from theories of empire (Kroneberg and

Wimmer 2012). Bendix traced how British elites rejected their traditional quasi-familial responsibilities for peasants and workers, promoting instead new ideologies of self-sufficiency for workers that were sometimes linked to market ideologies such as social Darwinism. This amounted to a form of abandonment of workers by their former privileged patrons; the response was that workers searched and struggled for new forms of political participation in an effort to secure benefits directly from the political center (Tilly 1995). But because mass political mobilization came after the construction of a modern administrative state that could accurately count populations and collect taxes, partisan patronage politics was less able to secure a foothold in the British system.

In the context of those Cold War debates over the prospects for democracy and dictatorship in the developing world, the political/combinatorial/sequential analyses of political sociologists provided an alternative to the "modernization" theory that informed both important academic debates and foreign policy strategies. Modernization arguments were, in a stylized way, a return to stage models of historical change but with an emphasis on the economic and cultural changes that pushed countries more or less quickly from one end of the spectrum to the other (for a review, see Roxborough 1988). As a guide to policy, these analyses provided support – intended or not by the scholars – for interventions designed to make societies more modern and, therefore, more prone to embrace democratic values, practices, and institutions. Specific interventions might involve educational programs and cultural festivals designed to exemplify freedom of speech or "individualism," efforts to promote voluntary associations or civic engagement, and, above all, policies designed to promote economic development and progress toward the development of free market capitalism.

In these debates, the policy goal was, above all, to avoid the alternative of revolution and, specifically, Communist revolution. But for political sociologists, revolution increasingly became a focus of theoretical and historical interest. What were the factors and conditions that led to the dramatic and sweeping social revolutions of the past – in France, Russia, and China – as well as the revolution that seemed to be multiplying across much of the world outside the industrial democracies during the 1960s and 1970s? These contemporary political events constituted a structure of relevance that prompted sociologists to engage intensively with the puzzles of revolutionary change as well as its absence.

Revolution as Regime Change

Systems of political power are confronted with changing conditions and challenges. Internally, social and economic developments may alter the relations among and conflicts between actors, thereby destabilizing political alliances. Externally, political orders may be challenged by other states or by broader patterns of global change. For political sociology, the key question is how do these two sources of pressure or disturbance produce distinctive patterns of change? To what extent are those patterns of change shaped by the existing political order and the possibilities for political participation, protest, and exit?

The first response to these questions turns on the observation that some social orders appear to be much more stable than others, which are marked by regular reorganization and reform. One of the earliest claims in what would become political sociology rested on just such a comparison between the reputed lack of dynamism that characterized "hydraulic societies" (dependent on large-scale irrigation with its requirement for centralized coordination to build and maintain systems) or "oriental despotism" (Wittfogel 1957). These characterizations of Asian social orders and empires, now very widely disputed, were used to set up a contrast with the claimed dynamism of ancient Mediterranean and European societies, a quality which featured centrally in narratives of the "rise of the West." The result of this stylized contrast, however, was an exercise in labeling societies as dynamic or not, rather than illuminating the conditions and processes that generate the reproduction or transformation of order. This recognition informs a change in focus, attending to specific forms of transformation and transition between regimes. As Michel Crozier, a French sociologist of organizations and politics wisely observed, "the pattern of change, and not the amount of change itself, must be considered as the basic variable" (1964: 226).

For political sociology, one pattern of response to the pressures of internal conflict and external challenge has been of particular theoretical importance: revolution. Whereas some revolutions, including the "bourgeois" revolutions in England (the Glorious Revolution of 1688) and what would become the United States (the War of Independence beginning in 1776), are predominantly political in that they produce changes in the forms of government or the identity of those who rule, social revolutions couple political change to broad transformations in the organization of social, economic, and cultural life. Given the dramatic character and expansive consequences of such revolutions – exemplified by the violent struggles and sweeping transformations of the French Revolution of 1789, the Russian Revolution of 1917, and the Chinese Revolution of 1949 – it is not surprising that many political sociologists have been drawn to the questions of what social conditions are associated with this pattern of intense, concentrated change (Goldstone 2001).

As with explanations of social change more generally, the social scientific study of revolution began with a descriptive analysis of stages of revolution (Brinton 1965). But engaged with both the work of scholars such as Barrington Moore and a vibrant literature of left-leaning social-political history, the focus of much inquiry shifted from the question of alternative paths – democracy or dictatorship? – to a direct engagement of specific cases of revolution with a set of expectations derived from the arguments of Karl Marx and Friedrich Engels. The questions frequently took the form of a set of anomalies (Calhoun 1983: 901–2). Why were peasants and artisans often central to revolutionary mobilizations, rather than the industrial proletariat (working class) that figured most prominently in Marxist theory? Why did the major revolutions in the name of socialism and communism occur in less-developed, agrarian societies (Russia and China in particular) rather than in the most industrialized societies where the immiseration and exploitation of the industrial working class would be expected to be greatest?

Among the most influential responses to the second question – why revolution had happened in less-developed societies – was Theda Skocpol's *States and Social Revolutions* (1979). Retaining Moore's attention to the configuration of different classes understood as political actors, she highlights the capacity of landed elites to frustrate government's capacity to address social grievances as well as the ways in which international factors – notably war and commercial competition – shape the state's capacity to contain grievances that might fuel insurrection and even revolution. On this point, the form of Skocpol's analysis of the sources of revolutionary situations resembles that of Barrington Moore with a number of critical differences. In place of the emergence of commercial agriculture, Skocpol highlights the pressures created by expanding circuits of international trade: "During these phases of global modernization, independent responses to the dilemmas posed by incorporation into a modernizing world were possible and (in some sense) necessary for governmental elites in agrarian bureaucracies" (1976: 180). A second key difference lies in the identity of the elites who take center stage: rather than alliances or competition between commercial and landed elites, Skocpol highlights relationships between governmental elites and those whose power and status came from massive agrarian holdings, often cemented by aristocratic status.

In *States and Social Revolution*, Skocpol's analysis centers on comparative levels of power: the power of the government elite versus that of the landed elites, the capacity of the government to contain dissent versus the extent of mobilization against elites and the states. But, as was discussed in the previous chapter, some forms of political ordering may be more or less capable of surviving rebellious and even revolutionary mobilization. In her analysis of empire as a political form, Karen Barkey highlighted how these "systems of rule ... lasted a long time mostly due to their flexibility and capacity to adapt and innovate" and their "robustness in the face of diversity, crisis, and change" (2008: 3). A rebellion in one province might unseat local notables, but would not so easily shake the center and spread to other provinces. In a centralized nation-state, unified by a culture of shared membership, it might be more difficult to mobilize a revolutionary movement but, if mobilized, that movement could well represent much more of a threat to the established order. Here again, we are reminded of a basic insight of political sociology: the features of an existing regime shape the possibilities for political action and, by extension, the likely trajectories of political change.

Whereas Skocpol's distinctive contribution was to focus attention on the varying capacity of the state to contain pressures and conflicts that might instigate revolution, another line of sociological research has focused on the factors that contribute to the capacity of revolutionary groups to mobilize and take advantage (intentionally or not) of the weakness of the state. Here, an important line of argument resonates with Michael Mann's model of the organization of power as constituted by the linkage of different kinds of social networks: ideological, economic, military, and political (see chapter 1). For scholars of revolution, a key question has been what social networks can be mobilized for – or "transposed" into (Sewell 1992) – insurgencies and, more generally, into what Charles Tilly (1995) has called "contentious politics."

This line of inquiry leads back to the first question posed by political sociologists as they turned their attention to revolution. The puzzle of unexpected revolutionaries, those radical peasants and artisans, inspired new forms of scholarship at the intersection of historical sociology and social history. Rather than seeing revolutionaries as the vanguard of a movement toward a socialist future, Craig Calhoun argued that "traditional communities provide the social foundations for widespread popular mobilizations and that traditional values provide their radicalism" (1983: 888), a pattern also evident in the key role of communal elites and appeals to religion and nationalism in mobilizations against authoritarian regimes throughout Southeast Asia (Slater 2009). Although Calhoun's framework of "tradition" and "modernity" pointed back to the post-Second World War cohort of historical and political sociologists, his focus on community relations and everyday social practices was in line with a pronounced shift occurring in the study of revolution. The insight that "communities provide the social foundations for widespread popularizations" heralded a turn toward the analysis of social networks in the study of revolutions.

In a comparative study of the revolution of 1848 in France and the Paris Commune of 1870, Roger Gould (1995) took this insight back to the original heartland for the sociology of revolutions: the urban working class. Although the central role of urban workers is consistent with the theoretical expectations of a broadly *marxisante* model of revolution, Gould argues that even workers did not automatically understand revolution as an expression of their interests. It was necessary for workers to settle "with increasing confidence on a singular and genuinely novel interpretation of the events," in which political mobilization came to be understood as "their revolution" which would be completed only with their enfranchisement and, by extension, a broader social revolution. The emergence of this new interpretation, as well as the mobilization that would follow, rested on the solidarities developed through co-residence in particular neighborhoods as well as the creation of "National Workshops ... within which the laboring poor of Paris could perceive themselves and each other for the first time as *workers*, pure and simple – not as plain citizens nor as shoemakers, stonemasons, or tailors, but as manual laborers" (1995: 33–4, 47).

Yet the emergence of this specific collective identity and understanding of interests was in no way guaranteed. The revolutionary forces mobilized out of the National Workshops confronted a counter-revolutionary "Mobile Guard." In his own account of 1848, *The Class Struggles in France* (Tucker 1978: 586–93), Karl Marx had attributed these differences to distinctive class bases: true proletarians or members of the working class in the National Workshops, *lumpenproletariat* or unskilled labor and those marginalized from the economy in the Mobile Guard. In a close study of the class location of those involved in these two organizational settings, Mark Traugott found no substantial differences. He argues instead that the comparative youth of those mobilized through the Guard made them particularly economically vulnerable in a time of high unemployment, whereas "insurgents tended to be longer-established practitioners of their trades, immersed in family, neighborhood, and professional networks to a greater extent." More significant, however, was the organizational character of the Mobile Guard in which "an officer corps dominated by professionals retained its coherence and managed to a considerable degree to isolate the rank and file from the civilian population" (Traugott 1980: 33, 38, 46; see also Gould 1995: 63–4). Across revolutions, routine democratic politics, and civic engagement (see chapter 4), the relational structure and culture within politically oriented organizations turn out to have profound effects on the character of those efforts (see Eliasoph 1998).

These analyses suggest that cross-cutting networks tend to increase the likelihood of mobilizing a successful insurgency. However, it is important to recognize that in many instances network ties can make participation less likely and generate pressures to refrain from insurgency. Jeff Goodwin illustrates this point with an analysis of the Huk Rebellion in the Philippines. Developing out of a Communist-led resistance against the Japanese Occupation during the Second World War, this wartime movement first mobilized to enter post-war elections. But when victorious candidates were prevented from entering the legislature and "attacks on the Huk veterans and the peasant movement increased in the months after the war," the resistance reorganized itself as the "People's Liberation Army," which required prolonging the absence of soldiers from kinship networks, marriages, and romantic relationships (1997: 57–8). The resulting "sex opportunism" strained commitments to the insurgency, raising "the possibility of divided emotional commitments that could weaken the Huk movement" (1997: 60). In her study of women's participation in the Civil War in El Salvador (see chapter 6), Jocelyn Viterna (2013) identifies similar dynamics at play in shaping patterns of recruitment into the guerrilla forces. Those women with robust family ties, either constrained by strong relations with parents or by commitments to children, were less likely to "go to the mountains." Instead, they tended to participate by providing information or acting as collaborators in their own villages.

These two approaches – centered on the capacity of the state to contain mobilization and the resources that social networks and settings provide for mobilization – are in no way incompatible, although the empirical demands of taking either approach create substantial challenges to combining both arguments. But given the rich secondary literature and wealth of archival data, John Markoff (1985) produced just such a combined analysis of the rural revolts that were an important part of the French Revolution of 1789. His findings underscored the *combinatorial* character of revolutionary processes just as Barrington Moore had developed a combinatorial account of democratization. The likelihood of rural revolt was influenced by processes of economic development and expansion of commercial networks, by the character and scope of central state control, and by the networks and institutions that shaped the capacity of subjects to resist the expansion of state power.

In the work of both Skocpol and Markoff, less emphasis is placed on the role of revolutionary ideologies and individual-level grievances than on economic relations and the repressive capacity of state structures. In these structural and network-based analyses, cultural factors may be necessary, but they are judged to be relatively weak in explaining why revolution happens in one place and not in another. Other scholars disagree, contending that ideology – and particularly the sense of an absence of legitimate rule – is a key factor in producing resistance and revolution, whether in nation-states or in state-like hierarchical organizations such as prisons (Goldstone and Useem 1999). But when it comes to understanding not just the occurrence of revolutions, but the question of who participates in revolutions with what consequences, questions of ideologies and grievances return to the forefront.

One starting point for such arguments is the recognition that revolutions are not independent of one another, particularly after the first wave of modern social revolutions. The great social revolutions that stand as independent "cases" in Skocpol's comparative analysis (1979) were present as cultural causal factors in later revolutionary episodes. The "constitutional" character of the French Revolution, with its establishment of a new representative assembly and laws, served to orient later revolutionaries in other countries to orient to different goals than those pursued by followers of the later non-constitutional Russian Revolution of 1917. These different models of political change, Nader Sohrabi (1995) argues, set different parameters for both mobilization of extra-legal resources and efforts to secure power through existing political institutions: "The revolutionaries, instead of demanding the complete and sudden overthrow of the old regimes, asked for the creation of an assembly by means of which they intended to render the traditional structures of rule ineffective. This path to power gave the constitutional revolutions an altogether different dynamic than revolutions that took place after the Russian Revolution of 1917" (1995: 1441).

A related puzzle can be found in the pattern of recruitment into the Chinese Communist Party out of a vibrant set of civic associations that were established during the era of the May Fourth Movement (1917–21). Here, the variation was not in the cultural message sent – first with the model of the French Revolution and then later with the different model of the Russian Revolution – but rather with the receptivity of different audiences. Why, Xiaohong Xu (2013) asks, did members of some of the 28 civic organizations under study respond to the recruitment efforts of the Communists while others did not? Comparing patterns of recruitment across organizations, Xu documents that the appeal was strongest in those groups that were already committed to "members' common pursuit of self-transformation" and which had "cultivated a sectarian culture of collective discipline and commitment and were cohesive enough to build up the consensus necessary to adopt a new form that demanded even *more* discipline and commitment" (Xu 2013: 776). Just as state-building projects promoted forms of discipline and self-cultivation that reinforced political order (see chapter 2; Gorski 2003; Ikegami 1995), so activists in pursuit of social change sought out recruits in organizational settings that possessed an "elective affinity" with the revolutionary movement.

By this point, the recursive quality of political ordering and political change should be clear. Through the processes of "social caging" and "social closure," networks built out of economic, ethnic, familial, and other relations are linked into systems of control that sustain relations of domination as well as the provision of shared social goods. At any given time and place, such structures may appear stable, but they are built out of intersecting networks that also represent opportunities for mobilizing to challenge and, possibly, to transform those political orders. The sociology of revolution focuses on one set of such challenges and has been most interested in the process by which political and social orders are destabilized. But, recalling the title of Barrington Moore's classic comparative study, what follows destabilization is also of interest: dictatorship or democracy? Before turning to sociological accounts of democratic politics – by far the largest component of political sociology in the United States and elsewhere – this chapter turns to a discussion of the alternative considered by Cold War scholars: the totalitarian path.

The Totalitarian Path

The sociological study of revolution, as we have seen, was shaped by a historically specific question about alternative paths of change: democracy or dictatorship? Although the two chapters that follow will focus on the democratic path, the odds of this outcome have lost the sense of inevitability that gathered strength at the end of the twentieth century. The claim that "there is no alternative" to democracy, made by British Prime Minister Margaret Thatcher in the 1980s, gained plausibility in the wake of the transition from fascism to democracy in Spain after Francisco Franco's death in 1975, the replacement of dictatorships by democratic governments in many Latin American countries during the 1980s and 1990s, the revolutions of 1989, including the transition from state socialism in Eastern Europe and the decomposition of the Soviet Union. A few decades later, however, democratic practices have eroded in many polities (Lachmann 2011), newly authoritarian leaders have appeared in many parts of the world, and even in long-established liberal democracy, basic rights and liberties appear under pressure. Thus before moving on to take a closer sociological look at democratic polities, it is important to understand the organizational and cultural character of the totalitarian alternative.

In one variant, totalitarianism may be understood as an extreme form of the centralized systems of direct rule described by Charles Tilly (1992; see chapter 1). In fictional form, these are the totalitarian dictatorships at the heart of George Orwell's *1984*, with omnipresent screens that both monitor and command individual subjects, or Kurt Vonnegut's (1988 [1968]) classic short story, "Harrison Bergeron," in which attractive people must be masked or maimed and the talented handicapped in order to ensure a government-imposed equality at the level of each individual. Sociologically, the equivalent of this image of imposed equality and identity is the state-led fragmentation of the social networks that might constitute a basis for autonomy from or resistance to centralized state power.

As a form of political order, totalitarianism also generates a characteristic "pattern of change" (Crozier 1964: 226). Such regimes are typically hostile to "intermediary organizations," a term that points to the capacity to organize around identities and networks at least somewhat independent of the state. In this respect, twentieth-century totalitarianism shared a governing precept known to rulers since ancient times. On this point, Michael Mann cites an exchange of letters between the Roman Emperor Trajan and a provincial governor who had requested permission to form fire brigades. A reasonable request in light of the recent devastation of an important city by fire, but Trajan refuses on the grounds that "this sort of society has greatly disturbed the peace .... . Whatever name we give them, and for whatever purposes they may be founded, they will not fail to form themselves into dangerous assemblies" (1986: 324).

In this spirit, although with a vastly different intensity, modern totalitarian regimes set to destroying or capturing associations that might threaten centralized control by the leadership. Under Mao, China undertook an even more dramatic project of erasing individual differences in dress and educational distinction, while enrolling the enormous population in state-directed mass organizations. As a consequence, major political disruptions such as the Cultural Revolution (1966–76) did not follow the lines of predetermined identities and interests that are already stabilized by intermediary organizations. Instead, alignments were an emergent property of conflicts within those mass organizations and major institutions, including schools and universities. As Andrew Walder has argued, "during the summer of 1966, the institutions that stabilized expectations about authority and linked one's status and position to political responses were breaking down rapidly in novel and unpredictable ways." Individuals were pressured to take stands which, inevitably, put them in opposition to those who took different stands. "The signals about expected behavior, very clear in stable circumstances, were suddenly scrambled. This divided those previously loyal to authority figures against one another in a conflict that generated new identities and urgent new interests" (2009: 12–13). Examining a later rupture of political control, the Tiananmen student movement of 1989, Dingxin Zhao provides a similar characterization of mobilization in a fragmented society with few networks capable of sustaining civic organization and political opposition: "The 1989 Movement tended to be driven by emotions, rumors, and traditional cultural elements exactly because it developed under an authoritarian state with higher state unity and the capacity to penetrate society, a society with very weak development of intermediate organizations, and a state legitimation based on moral and economic performance" (2001: 355).

In contrast to the omnipresent centralized state, a second variant of totalitarianism rests on the capture of civil society by the state. This is the fascist alternative. As Dylan Riley argues, fascism overturns a core assumption of Tocqueville's analysis of the importance of civil society to political development. Whereas Tocqueville argued that it was the strength of associations outside the state that kept the development of a strong administrative state in check (and, thereby, limited the threats that such a strong state would pose to democracy), Riley builds on an observation by the Italian political philosopher Antonio Gramsci (1891–1937) and argues that "strong associational spheres can enable hegemonic authoritarian regimes to the extent that associations provide a congenial environment for the construction of authoritarian parties" (2005: 290). This model rejected an understanding of politics as a contest between organized groups external to the state and, instead, positioned civic associations as both recruiting grounds for the party-state and as instrumentalities for the implementation of state policy and the multiplication of the state's capacity for surveillance and coercion.

Across these variations on the totalitarian state, the relation of "state" and "society" is analytically central (Zhao 2001). Restated in the theoretical imagery with which we began, one of the key features of totalitarian regimes is a profound asymmetry in the development of networks and organizational capacity. Whereas Tocqueville's ideal of democratic society as a bulwark against the development of a despotic administrative state required strong civic associations, powerful totalitarian regimes are constituted in conditions where networks that could sustain alternative factions are weak. Yet, even in such institutional settings, many of the basic elements of political action and possibilities for change are still evident.

Taking on the puzzle of East Germany's ten-week passage from seemingly solid authoritarian regime to the fall of the government and opening of the Berlin Wall in November 1989, Steven Pfaff and Hyojoung Kim focus on the intersection of knowledge about the distribution of grievances and the structure of the networks through which knowledge flows and which, like the traditional communities of Calhoun's reactionary radicals, provide an infrastructure for mobilization to seize a moment of perceived weakness on the part of the authorities. Their argument begins by recognizing the extraordinary surveillance capacity of the East German state and how it shaped the possibilities for political mobilization: "Even in repressive mono-organizational regimes, general knowledge of the state's poor performance is not difficult for citizens to obtain. What is often left secret is how widely grievances are *shared* among one's neighbors, particularly where extralocal communication is difficult.... In the absence of such information, individual grievances remain too compartmentalized to fuel collective action" (2003: 408).

The capacity of this state surveillance system was challenged both by events in other nations – notably the "ten years" of mobilization by "Solidarity" in Poland – and the mismatch of technology and territory. Many on the western fringe of East Germany were exposed to television broadcasts from West Germany and, of course, news also flowed through other more or less covert channels. Thus, when news came that holidaymakers in the state-socialist country of Czechoslovakia were able to leave from there for Western Europe, a stream of those seeking opportunities for "exit" rapidly gathered momentum.

These exits, in turn, catalyzed other action, overcoming some of the fragmentation produced by surveillance and a lack of information about the grievances of others. Quoting the economist Thomas Schelling, Pfaff and Kim explain that "The role of 'incidents' can thus be seen as a coordinating role; it is a substitute for overt leadership and communication. Without something like an incident, it may be difficult to get action at all" (Pfaff and Kim 2003: 409). But the action, in this case exit, was most likely to come from those who were also the most obvious leaders for a political mobilization within East Germany: "Early exiters are more likely to come from those discontented persons with the least degree of loyalty to the state ... In sufficient degree exit becomes so generalized that highly aggrieved but partially loyal citizens may also leave the country. These defections would be a devastating blow to movement prospects" (2003: 413).

Here again, the recursive processes of political ordering and contesting order are evident. Social networks provide some of the most important material for the construction of stable systems of centralized power and control. But the ways in which power and control are organized act back upon society, sometimes to strengthen and sometimes to erode the practices and patterns of social relationships upon which they were initially built. Across the varieties of totalitarian regimes, this has tended to produce strongly centralized systems of direct rule and weak bases for opposition; but when mobilization develops – as fever, rumor, or emergent system of opposition – then these seemingly strong regimes sometimes prove to be surprisingly brittle.

In response to the efforts by elites and states to contain the expression of grievances and political mobilization, actors – individual or collective – may respond in a variety of ways, including the exercise of "exit" and "voice" (Hirschman 1970; see chapter 1). Exit may entail actual departure and escape from a given "social cage." Alternatively, the mobilization of grievances in the form of voice may lead to calls for the destruction of the existing social order. The balance of these two options, combined with the force of loyalty to existing arrangements, shapes the probabilities of different responses to the political containment of grievances.

The diverging paths of dictatorship and democracy over the past centuries cannot be reversed, but they are always potentially vulnerable to redirection under the pressure of internal dissatisfaction or conflict as well as external pressures and opportunities. Recent decades have seen particularly dramatic reversals on what was once the totalitarian side of the ledger, with the replacement of many state socialist regimes by electoral democracies. The journalist Timothy Garton Ash (1990) summed up the dramatic changes of 1989 with the observation that "In Poland it took ten years, in Hungary ten months, in Germany ten weeks" before hoping that the political transformation in Czechoslovakia would be more rapid still. But those concerned with the stability of democracies should not be complacent. These regimes also require the reproduction and transformation of social networks and shared identities, both of which are vulnerable to erosion or capture by other political dynamics. Surveying the present – as well as possible future – prospects for democratic governance, we need to understand how this particular kind of political regime functions in order to preserve and strengthen its core values of liberty, equality, and popular sovereignty.

4
Voice and Vote in Democratic Politics

Democratic politics pose a strong analytic challenge to sociology. This challenge is particularly great when the task is to make sense of liberal democracy in sociological terms. To the extent that the principles of a specifically liberal polity begin with the rights-bearing, rational, and self-sufficient citizen, then social networks, interactions, emergent properties, and shared cultural frameworks are pushed into the background and, at times, entirely obscured. Instead, the focus is on individual deliberation and choice, exercised in the decisions about whether to vote, how to vote, or whether to replace voting with some other form of political participation.

Early modern political theory began with precisely such an image of the individual. Recall that hypothetical situation discussed by Rousseau (chapter 1). One person is taken captive by another. The captor must constantly guard his prisoner; the captive looks for any opportunity to whack his captor over the head and escape into the forest. Here, there are no pre-existing social ties, but rather two individuals in what the contract theorist Thomas Hobbes (1588–1679) described as the "state of nature" which was also presumed to be a "state of war." With this starting point, the central question concerned the conditions under which these rights-bearing but asocial individuals would agree to give up their natural rights in return for the security provided by a sovereign power. The central mechanism for producing such a social order was the concept of a "social contract."

This theoretical project envisions social order as created through the consent of already independent individuals bearing rights given by nature and possessed of the capacity for reason. This way of thinking is foundational to the kind of democratic regimes that have come to be taken for granted in many parts of the modern world. These assumptions, shared by many of the theorists who worked to imagine a form of political order that was not monarchy legitimated by divine right, continue to influence the ways in which we think about politics, both as academics and as citizens. Just as fish are sometimes said to have no concept of water, as well-socialized members of liberal democratic regimes, it is often difficult for us to look beyond individual citizens in order to see the networks and social cages and patterns of social closure that inform so much political sociology of the pre-democratic and non-democratic worlds.

One of the most celebrated theorists of American democracy demonstrated how the social and relational dimensions of political life are smuggled in after the assumption of the individual-as-actor is established. In his famous chapter "On Political Association in the United States," Alexis de Tocqueville starts by asserting that "Americans are taught from birth that they must overcome life's woes and impediments on their own. Social authority makes them mistrustful and anxious, and they rely upon its power only when they cannot do without it." But this strong vision of individualism is immediately qualified: "An obstruction blocks a public road, interrupting the flow of traffic. The neighbors immediately set up a deliberative body. Out of this improvised assembly comes an executive power that will remedy the ill before it occurs to anyone to appeal to an authority prior to that of the interested parties" (2004: 215). This political alchemy, by which deeply individualistic selves engage in collaboration to preempt the action of some agent of central government, can be easily overshadowed by that initial assertion of individualism and liberty as core political values.

In order to recover the sociology in modern democratic politics, it is necessary to begin by rethinking this image of the calculating, deciding individual voter and ask questions that probe more deeply into how such citizens are socially constituted. We must explore how the set of choices they face – and the resources with which they face them – are products of distinctive social contexts and social processes. Whereas earlier chapters focused on the articulation of social networks into distinctive political orders, the sociology of democracy requires a more intense focus on individuals as they are embedded in multiple networks and institutionally constituted as "independent" decision-makers.

As with the preceding chapter on regimes and revolutions, we begin in the world of American sociology immediately after the Second World War. While some scholars were engaged in the comparative project of understanding the pathways to dictatorship and democracy, others turned their investigations to the operation of American democracy, which they understood to be an exemplar and, therefore, a model to which other nations could and should aspire.

The Sociological Model of Voting

In this liberal understanding of democracy, elections were a central element and, therefore, one of the puzzles was why people voted the way they did. In the aftermath of the Second World War, social scientists were keenly aware that Adolph Hitler had been elected to high office in Germany, even if the events by which he came to occupy the highest office were more opaque and menacing. They also remembered the key role of military veterans in the elections that gave rise to the fascist regime in Italy under Benito Mussolini. The fact that both of the most recent paths taken to totalitarianism in Western Europe began with electoral victories meant that elections in and of themselves were no guarantee of durable democracy. It was necessary to understand why people voted the way that they did – if, indeed, they voted at all.

The sociological approach to the explanation of voting behavior came of age with the development of public opinion polling and survey research. The first large-scale opinion polling operations were founded in the mid-1930s, notably both Gallup and Roper (Igo 2007), and this approach to research gained further credibility in both academic and policy schools with major studies during the Second World War, exemplified by Samuel Stouffer's *The American Soldier*, a contribution to a broad effort to understand and evaluate the war effort in terms of social psychology and organizational dynamics (Ryan 2012). Surveys organize information about the political world in a distinctive way. The unit of measurement is the individual informant to whom are attached a set of attributes (age, gender, occupation, educational level, income, race, religion, etc.) and a set of preferences, opinions, and reports of behavior.

Although post-war political sociologists sometimes framed their questions in terms of relationships, asking about the influence of community leaders on other voters (Lazarsfeld et al. 1944), much of the theoretical work linked these attributes to assumptions about group membership (Berelson et al. 1954). Working from an assumption of "homophily" (the principle that "birds of a feather flock together"), this line of argument envisioned the individuals who responded to surveys as belonging to different groups or categories: families, occupational groups, religious congregations, and leisure activities. By virtue of the "groups" that were understood as the source of different identities or attributes, individuals were assumed to come into contact and conversation with others who shared their attitudes and political preferences. This insight generated at least two distinct lines of scholarship pursued by political sociologists and political scientists alike. One, profoundly comparative in nature, sought to identify the distinctiveness of American democracy (among others) in terms of each country's particular set of cross-cutting or aligned associational memberships (Almond and Verba 1965; Lipset and Rokkan 1967; Schattschneider 1960). A second sought to identify the relative strength of these different social attitudes in shaping the decision to vote one way or another, to join one party or another. As methods of survey research were harnessed to new technologies of regression analysis, this second research agenda came to define the "sociological model of voting."

We have already encountered a pre-democratic version of this model in those theories of revolution which begin by identifying different classes and their economically given interests (chapter 3). Recall how scholars such as Barrington Moore made sense of political trajectories toward democracy and dictatorship by identifying different configurations and alliances among landed elites, peasants, merchants, and urban workers – economic "groups" that were assumed to map onto different interests and grievances. Carried over to the study of democratic politics, this "structural" perspective created expectations that party loyalty and voting behavior would be similarly driven by the economic location of individual citizens. To understand these outcomes, researchers responded with more complex models in which "social structural variables, including class origins and occupation, were seen as operating at the mouth of the funnel, leading to the social-psychological attributes (primarily political attitudes and partisan identification) at the narrow end of the funnel that ultimately predicted vote choice" (Manza et al. 1995: 140; for the original statement of the "funnel of causality," see Campbell et al. 1960). Although this pattern could be found in a number of European systems where party identity mapped more explicitly on to class (a topic for chapter 5), researchers found that often class provided surprisingly weak explanatory purchase on opinion and voting behavior.

To make sense of this unexpected absence of a strong association between structural or socio-economic location and political actions, political sociologists and political scientists have developed a number of theoretical alternatives. In some, the weak and weakening relationship between voting and class location is attributed to processes that in a sense "liberate" individuals from their class context: "embourgeoisement" or social mobility, processes of political learning through which "the increased capacity of a better-educated citizenry to make political decisions [becomes] independent of the constraints of class loyalty or other social attributes" (Manza et al. 1995: 144). Others have pointed to the emergence of a new set of "post-materialist" values associated with the environmental and gay rights movements or the heightened salience of identities other than class, including those grounded in gender, race, and religion. Finally, still other scholars argue that broad changes in the organization and character of the economy have altered the electoral calculus of individuals, as they think of themselves as consumers, or debtors, or current and future recipients of government benefits. At the end of their literature review, Manza et al. come to a modest conclusion: "At this juncture only one conclusion is firm: In no democratic capitalist country has vote been entirely independent of class in a national election" (1995: 158).

Yet class – often operationalized as income or occupation, which are not quite the same concepts – has proved to be both indispensable and insufficient to explain political participation. In an important effort to untangle these puzzles at least for patterns of political participation in the United States, a trio of political scientists – Sidney Verba, Kay Lehman Schlozman, and Henry Brady (1995) – conducted a major survey, the Civic Engagement Project. Their goal was to understand the determinants of a wide range of political behavior including volunteering, writing letters to editors or officials, and engaging in protest. Their analysis helps to clarify the puzzling role of socio-economic background in explaining political behavior. Rather than operating as a discrete factor, socio-economic status (SES) operates along multiple paths or "sets of participatory factors [that] are, in fact, interwoven: initial advantages with respect to resources are associated with psychological engagement in politics and with placement in networks of political recruitment" (1995: 20). Because each of these factors – resources, engagement, recruitment – can also be shaped by influences other than family background such as attending church, belonging to a union, or pursuing higher education, the pure explanatory power of SES is often muted. Although this rich mix of social contexts and personal ties may be important for many political behaviors, these factors seem not to predict who will make political donations. For this political act, family income alone mattered (1995: 28).

Although the debates over the determinants of voting behavior continue, these models tend to share a particular imagery of how politics works. The key insight is that individual preferences and actions, including voting, are "inputs" into a political system that produces a specific kind of "output" in the form of public policies and services. The next chapter will introduce challenges to this framework, which highlight how preferences and actions are themselves the products of public policy. But before taking that step, this chapter surveys a number of sociological approaches to the study of political participation: political socialization, organizational vehicles for participation, and cultural or cognitive approaches to the formation of preferences and understanding of interests. These arguments are paired with explanations for why people do not participate, including institutional structures of exclusion such as disenfranchisement, and the conditions for "rational apathy" even among those with an unquestioned right to vote and participate.

Political Socialization and the Constitution of Citizens

Just as political regimes have sought to cultivate subjects who will be obedient and disciplined (see chapter 2), democratic regimes endure to the extent that they are embedded in social worlds that constitute citizens of a most distinctive type. If different kinds of regimes *assume* distinctive understandings of the individual (e.g. as rights-bearing, as motivated by interests or loyalties, etc.), different kinds of political order also produce distinctive kinds of people. The experience of being born into a society with a particular kind of organization (or choosing to relocate later in life) involves exposure to characteristic processes of *political socialization*. The power of this influence is suggested by the repeated finding that one of the best predictors of one's identification with a political party is one's parents' party identification (Neuman 1986: 95–6), although recent research has documented the importance of children's perceptions – correct or incorrect – of their parents' partisan loyalties (Ojeda and Hatemi 2015). Similarly strong and durable effects on political culture have been demonstrated for religious and ethnic traditions (Elazar 1975).

Family, class, and religious culture were at the forefront of the first generation of post-war research on partisan identification and political socialization. But that post-war era also saw the proliferation of new forms of political influence, as television added its force to newspapers and radio as a potential factor in shaping political orientations and preferences on specific issues. Despite popular claims that increased polarization among elites and in media coverage of politics has produced parallel polarization in the electorate, evidence for such a causal connection has proven elusive (Fiorina and Abrams 2008; Prior 2013). The opposite causal claim – that increasingly extreme media represents a response to polarization in the electorate – has also failed to receive wide support. Instead, some scholars point to the changing technologies and economic incentives to account for the rise of predominantly conservative talk radio (Berry and Sobieraj 2011). But, as will become evident when the discussion turns to political parties (chapter 5) and social movements (chapter 6), media framing can have potent effects on citizens' knowledge, preferences, and propensity to participate in specific contexts.

Political socialization goes far deeper than partisan identification and media exposure. As Alexis de Tocqueville observed of the early nineteenth-century United States, children learned basic democratic skills in the games that they played. Later in that century, many schools were organized according to an American version of what was known as the "Lancastrian" model. One student was selected to supervise the entire, often very large, class for a limited period of time. Once that week or month or term was up, the student supervisor would then become one of the supervised (Baker 1983: 92–4). So the practice of rotation in office – a basic precept of electoral democracy – was expected to teach students to exercise their power responsibly and justly so that they would not be subject to retribution when they returned to their status as just another member of the class.

Because basic forms of social relations are defined by the presence of hierarchy and a characteristic division of labor, almost any social setting can be a context for learning how to do a particular kind of politics and be a particular kind of citizen. As a rich historical and ethnographic literature has documented, different kinds of organizations and movements reproduce specific ways of understanding oneself as political and carry different models of public identity. These insights are closely tied to the claims made for the importance of civil society – the privately organized but publicly oriented sphere of discourse and action (see chapter 1). A famous example from Tocqueville's *Democracy in America* makes the basic point. Marveling at the phenomenon of a national association organized to contest tariff laws in the 1830s, he argued that association served as a medium in which individuals not only clarified their own preferences but gained evidence of the extent to which their opinions were more widely held. In contrast to the ways in which East Germany's totalitarian regime made it difficult for individuals to judge whether or not others shared their grievances (chapter 3), "In America, citizens of the minority associate primarily to ascertain their numerical strength and thereby weaken the moral ascendancy of the majority" as well as to promote "competition among ideas" that will identify the arguments most likely to persuade those of the majority (2004: 218–20). To the extent that such associations serve as schools of citizenship, citizens learn to argue, to evaluate arguments, and to have patience that good arguments will build majorities that will then be expressed through democratic elections.

In other organizational settings, however, individuals may learn more complex lessons and be constituted as citizens in self-contradictory ways. In a study of nonprofit organizations working with youth, Nina Eliasoph documents the prevalence of a particular model which she terms "the empowerment project" which uses "a complex mix of government, nonprofit, and private funds to transform whole groups of people's personal feelings and sense of self, to cure them of their social ills by 'empowering' them. These projects' goal is to bring people closer to government, to bring people closer to each other, so that the participants can make decisions in a democratic way" (2011: 4). Perversely, however, by making people take responsibility for their own problems – and thereby come to understand themselves *as* the problem even when those problems are the result of deeply entrenched systems of inequality – such "empowerment projects" may both provide opportunities for democratic socialization and demonstrations of its limitations, even impotence.

The power of this analysis lies in its linking of the patterns of interaction or "etiquettes" (Eliasoph 1998) embedded in different kinds of organizations with their consequences for the formation of selves and mastery of skills and orientations that may have political implications. If the "empowerment projects" advanced by some social welfare nonprofits turn out to undercut their own goals at times, other arrangements in other places may set more productive dynamics in motion. As Carmen Sirianni has documented in his research on public participation in watershed management, federal agencies such as the Environmental Protection Agency are able to "engage in shared cognitive reframing of public problems with ordinary citizens and civic associations, coproduce usable tools to assist collaborative problem solving, help build networks that can leverage trust and learning on a broad scale, and align collaborative and deliberative tools" with the more bureaucratic and technocratic practices of federal governance (2014: 227). With this focus on the relationship between the organization of political practices and the constitution of civic actors, there is a theoretical affinity between the organizational analyses of participatory politics and historical studies inspired by Foucault (e.g. Gorski 2003; Ikegami 1995) that excavate specifically political projects of creating disciplined selves. But there are high stakes in linking the two inasmuch as this connection undercuts the presumption that civil society – the realm of publicly oriented but privately managed association – is a domain that is independent of the state, sustains criticism of the state, and cultivates the capacity to mobilize independent and even oppositional political action.

This question of whether civic associations are consistently "civic" with respect to cultivating skills and patterns of engaged participation has inspired a lively exchange between political sociology and organizational analysis. Recognizing that models of organization are themselves constitutive of claims to political identity and ideals of political order (Clemens 1996), studies of social movement organizations and new forms of civic association (Lee 2015; Polletta 2002; see chapter 6) have explored how organization shapes political life. Here, as in Eliasoph's analysis of "empowerment projects," the findings suggest the difficulties of directly cultivating democratic practice. In *Do-It-Yourself Democracy*, for example, Caroline Lee (2015) studies the dialogue-and-deliberation industry. Although the name may be unfamiliar, the practices are not. Gather concerned citizens and stakeholders in a large convention hall – in Houston, refugees from New Orleans after Hurricane Katrina; in Manhattan, residents and business owners who contemplate a post-9/11 city. Then arrange them around tables to generate ideas in response to a set of prompts or questions provided by the organizers. Moderators collect feedback, display the emerging "consensus" on large pads of paper propped up on easels or PowerPoint slides updated by an assistant. The cumulative results of such gatherings are then analyzed and arrayed by consultants and presented to the agencies or organizations that commissioned the "visioning" effort in the first place. Through a combination of participant-observation (both at conferences and training courses), interviews, archival work, and a survey done in collaboration with other researchers, Lee traces the roots of these practices in both the broad counter-culture of the 1960s and 1970s as well as in corporate management techniques. But her analysis goes beyond genealogy to document the constitution of a new professional identity and industry as well as to illuminate how these professional models function to manage tensions within contemporary politics, specifically a moment of fiscal scarcity and a need to manage citizens as "customers" of government. Those who commission deliberative exercises often influence the framing of questions and the structure of options presented to participants. For participants, the experience may be empowering in the moment but disconnected from the networks of mobilization that would be necessary for translating the experience of deliberation into effective political action.

Studies of political socialization, whether in families, schools or civic associations, illuminate the processes of constituting capable and skilled citizens – or not. But the exercise of these capacities for democratic participation also requires organizational settings that harness such political socialization to forms of mobilization that have the capacity to exert meaningful pressure on political decision-makers and help to shape political agendas. In some cases, the interaction context may promote democratic skills only to have these new expectations dashed by the lack of a meaningful and substantial connection between the experience of participation and its consequences for policies. In other contexts, the organization of participation may be tied to substantive influence over meaningful outcomes, producing a virtuous cycle which encourages further participation and greater investment in civic engagement by government agencies. But such opportunities to participate in policy formation are not always – or even often – created at the initiatives of those who already hold power. To connect participation and policy, citizens and activists have discovered and invented new forms of collective mobilization, thereby building a rich "repertoire of contention" or "organizational repertoire" (Clemens 1993; Tilly 1995) for democratic politics.

Organizational Repertoires

By participating in groups, people develop ties to others. As many scholars have documented, the quantity and quality of network ties – or "social capital" – are important for both the capacity of individuals to participate successfully in institutionalized politics and to be mobilized into effective contentious politics (Putnam 2000). Consequently, one of the most important effects of different political regimes lies in their capacity to cultivate or obstruct the development of social ties within and between different categories of citizens. Regimes may encourage the widespread formation of cross-cutting ties by promoting freedom of association or limit the existence of autonomous groups and thereby the social makings of civic mobilization as is often the case under totalitarian regimes (see chapter 3). In other cases, the distribution of rights of access may encourage development of ties within, rather than between, groups. The organization of rule as well as the structure of social lives contributes to how people understand themselves as political actors and the patterns of their mobilization to shape political outcomes.

But just as those building political orders have drawn on a wide range of social networks to construct systems of rule, those who seek to influence politics can be similarly creative in discovering new models for organizing collective action. Even if democratic political systems are often unresponsive to voter preferences, there are cases in which relatively powerless or disadvantaged citizens discover ways in which to mobilize effectively to secure political rights, influence, and benefits. In *The People's Lobby* (1997), Elisabeth Clemens explored one such period in American political development: the mobilization of large, mass membership voluntary associations in electoral and legislative politics in the late nineteenth and early twentieth centuries. Looking across the efforts by farmers' associations, organized labor, and women's groups that defined both the populism of the 1890s and the progressivism of the next two decades, Clemens observed an unexpected pattern. Contrary to assumptions that those with the most resources, rights, and numbers would enjoy the most political success, the reverse was true. Although they lacked the vote and cultural legitimacy as political actors along with access to financial resources, organized women succeeded in gaining the vote for themselves and playing an important role in depriving enfranchised men of the right to drink. Organized labor, by comparison, met with much fiercer and more successful opposition.

Comparing mobilizing efforts and outcomes across a number of states with a reputation for progressive politics, Clemens argued that relatively disadvantaged political actors gained influence by discovering new ways of organizing. These new models often involved the *transposition* of organizational forms from one social domain or field to another (Sewell 1992). Women organized *as if* they were a business enterprise to circumvent the proscriptions of strongly gendered forms of politics; farmers and industrial workers organized *as if* they were a fraternal society in order to draw on cultural models of solidarity in an era of ruthlessly competitive capitalism. Taking advantage of a well-established civil society – complete with multiple newspapers and lecture circuits as well as an expansive system of public education open to the organized influence of social movements – mobilized interest groups were able to get issues on the agenda (Gaventa's second level of power) and, in the longer run, to change preferences through formal and informal education that turned dangers that had seemed inevitable into problems that could be solved.

This capacity of comparatively disadvantaged actors – whether in terms of economic standing, gender, age, race, or any other basis of political exclusion – to improvise with social materials that are not already recognized as explicitly political is an important source of social movement mobilization and political change. These dynamics will be explored at greater length in chapter 6, but it is important not to be swept away in a celebration of the power of political innovation and entrepreneurship. The initial prompt to be creative about political organizing is often the product of deep, durable, and damaging systems of political oppression and exclusion. Even in regimes that officially celebrate democratic values and participation, such processes of exclusion of actors as well as issues operate to create specifically political dimensions or intensifications of inequality.

Structuring the Electorate: Institutional Limits on Political Participation

As we have learned from the discussion of political socialization, family upbringing and everyday life help to shape the attitudes, skills and values that people may – or may not – bring to active political participation. But although no one can truly escape politics in the broad sense, actual participation in organized political life is far from universal. Some of the most important questions in political sociology address who participates and why. Just as importantly, we need to understand why some do not participate and why not.

One set of answers to these questions focuses on the rules governing rights of participation. Even though the American Revolution is accurately described as a *democratic* revolution, it ushered in a significantly limited sort of democracy. The right to vote was limited in multiple ways, from state to state, town to town, and between state and federal elections. But the general pattern was that the vote was limited to adult white men, sometimes to those who were either native-born or had resided in the country for some set number of years, and sometimes to those who owned property. This last qualification endured particularly in local elections concerned with property taxation. Women were usually excluded, although sometimes not when they owned property in their own name. African Americans, Native Americans, other minorities, recent immigrants (although how recent varied), felons, lunatics, and paupers were also often denied suffrage rights. Starting from this point, many histories of American politics are organized in terms of the gradual and contested extension of the right to vote. In other nations, however, basic forms of political participation are mandatory. In Belgium, Turkey, and Australia, for example, voting is legally required, producing turnout rates of 80–90 percent in recent elections in contrast to the turnouts of 50 to not quite 60 percent in recent American presidential elections (DeSilver 2015).

This history of democratic exclusions can be understood in terms of the relational models that are central to the construction of political order. To the extent that democracies, like other systems of order, are built out of social networks that are not necessarily democratic, they will incorporate inegalitarian elements. Consider some of the attributes that have limited even the rights of white men to vote: they are often required to have reached some age, typically understood as equivalent to adulthood with its implications of marriage and parenthood; sometimes they have been required to be property holders; in a number of American states during the nineteenth century, paupers were disenfranchised even if they were adult, married, white men. Sometimes, very fine distinctions were drawn: residents of poor houses who did household work in return for their board were considered enfranchised; those who were entirely dependent were prevented from voting (Keyssar 2000: 61).

The equality of adult white men is thus built upon a set of what political theorist Rogers Smith (1993) identifies as "ascriptive" hierarchies, notably of gender and race but also employment status (the exclusion of dependents of which paupers were an important subclass). In Europe and North America, therefore, the history of democracy is often written as one of gradual extension of full, enfranchised citizenship, a process that has followed different paths and proceeded at different rates. In Britain, for example, there was almost a century of struggle to expand the right to vote among men based on ever lower property qualifications; only in 1918 was the vote extended to all men over 21 and to a large number of women over 30. Equalization of the voting age for men and women took another decade. In France, by contrast, the legacy of the Revolution was universal male suffrage in 1792; women did not achieve the same political standing until 1944. In both cases, the fact that the nation-state was also the central state of an empire (chapter 2) meant that "universal" might – or might not – be qualified in terms of place of birth, race, or ethnicity.

In the United States, a historically novel organizational form – the national social movement (Young 2006) – supported two major mobilizations for the extension of the suffrage along with a host of related demands. Sometimes operating in parallel or in alliance or at cross-purposes, the abolitionist movement against slavery and the women's rights movement provide powerful examples of how those who are excluded from participation in the polity (Gaventa's second dimension of power) can creatively find new spaces and means for political mobilization (see chapter 6). Although the story of all these emancipatory movements – for civil rights, for women's rights, for the enfranchisement of immigrants – is often structured as if the endpoint will be some form of full and equal political participation, the current state of the electorate in the United States calls this expectation into question. The electoral victories of Jacksonian democracy in the early nineteenth century ushered in decades of high voter turn-out among those white adult men who could vote, a pattern that held most strongly in northern states. White men in the south turned out at lower rates. As the vote was extended by law and then in actuality to African American men, the participation of those who had just gained the vote was lower still, reflecting a combination of intimidation at the polls and low expectations about if and how votes would matter. A similar pattern followed the federal amendment granting all adult women the right to vote in 1920 and the extension of the vote to 18–21 year olds in 1971 (Rosenstone and Hansen 1993). Over time, however, increasing diversity in the pool of candidates as well as shifts in the concerns that drive voters to the polls have produced greater variation in turn-out rates across different demographic categories (Burns et al. 2001).

This puzzle about non-voting becomes still stranger in light of evidence about who votes. Those who describe themselves as "likely voters" in public opinion surveys are more than 10 percent more likely to state that they would prefer "lower taxes and fewer services" rather than the reverse. Those who are not registered to vote, by comparison, prefer "higher taxes and more services" than less of each by an even greater margin (McElwee 2014; Page et al. 2013). Whereas a model of the rational voter or "pocketbook politics" might predict that those who most want government services would be most likely to mobilize to get them, the reverse is much more likely – particularly in a mid-term rather than presidential election.

What explains this puzzling pattern? A part of the answer can be found in the process by which issues are understood as "close to home" (Eliasoph 1997) or far away. Those with higher incomes and more wealth are more attuned to the impact of the tax system on their immediate well-being and, as we will see in the next chapter, less likely to recognize the benefits that they receive from government programs as government services. A second source of these patterns of voting and not-voting lies in the technical requirements of exercising the vote. An extreme example of these hurdles is found in the efforts of African Americans to vote in southern states prior to the successes of the civil rights movement. While formally entitled to the vote, to exercise the vote African Americans had to register to vote, a seemingly technical requirement that allowed state and local officials to police – sometimes bureaucratically, sometimes aided by the application of coercion – access to political participation (Morris 1993). Some of the most dramatic scenes of the civil rights struggle in the American South centered on the courage required for African Americans to attempt to register to vote and the many obstacles, threats, and reprisals that were so often involved (Payne 1995). The power of local bureaucrats and officials to interpret and control the implementation of the law has led to new waves of mobilization that focus on the "fine print" of political equality. A particularly strong example of this strategy can be found in the "Motor Voter Law" of 1993. Championed by Frances Fox Piven and Richard Cloward – whose careers encompassed sociology, political science, social policy implementation and activism – this electoral reform expanded their long-standing concern with the capacity of the poor to mobilize political influence through protest or the fiscal pressure of social services and into a strategy for increasing participation at the voting booth (Piven and Cloward 1977). The law required state officials to provide voter registration materials to eligible citizens when they applied for a driver's license or some form of public assistance (Piven and Cloward 2000). Even here, a seemingly egalitarian opportunity to register may introduce new forms of inequality, particularly with respect to difficulties of access to such facilities by those without cars or nearby public transportation. However broad the concept of equality enshrined in the right to vote, the details of implementation retain the capacity to inject new dimensions of inequality.

One of the most powerful instances of this dynamic in the United States is evident in the dramatic growth of felon disenfranchisement over recent decades. The basic claim that those who have committed serious crimes should not be treated as full citizens is not new; felons were listed along with women, children, morons, slaves, and Native Americans as those not qualified to vote in the early American Republic (Keyssar 2000). What has changed, instead, is the rate of conviction and imprisonment as well as the extension of disenfranchisement after someone has served their full sentence. The implications of these developments for political equality are even more troubling, as the increase in incarceration has been felt most severely by African American men.

The racial dimension of felon disenfranchisement is evident in the timing of the adoption of laws. Roughly one-third of states had some such exclusion on the books in the 1840s; by the 1870s and 1880s, over 80 percent of states limited the voting rights of felons and, by 2000, this proportion was over 90 percent (Manza and Uggen 2004: 493). With this structure of exclusion in place in state law, the onset of the "war on crime" and "war on drugs" in the 1960s and 1970s triggered a powerful interaction process. Dramatic increases in incarceration, disproportionately involving men of color (Alexander 2010; Fortner 2015; Weaver and Lerman 2010), set off a process whereby important electoral gains made by the civil rights movement were undercut by restrictions on the electorate in minority communities through the impact of the criminal justice system (Uggen and Manza 2002), and further reinforced by the effects of mass incarceration on employment opportunities and, therefore, on the economic resources of many communities of color.

Although these restrictions take their starkest form in the case of felon disenfranchisement, the organization of registration and balloting structures the electorate with respect to other demographic groups. College students, for example, may face particular challenges when it comes to establishing residency (Lieberman 2012). The elderly and poor may be less likely to exercise the vote when official identification cards are required and are available only from government offices that may require help with transportation or significant waits during working hours. As we shall see in the next chapter, these impacts of policy on the capacity and motivation to participate in politics can have consequential effects on political outcomes. Policies and public programs can be designed in ways that make it more or less likely that citizens will recognize those benefits as political and, therefore, as legitimate targets for mobilization and lobbying.

Rational Apathy

Recognizing the many ways in which the interests, preferences, and organizational capacities of democratic citizens are shaped by social processes that often go unrecognized, one is left with a troubling question. Are there good reasons that democratic citizens opt out of democratic participation? Are voters correct in believing themselves to be relatively power-less? In *Affluence and Influence: Economic Inequality and Political Power in America*, political scientist Martin Gilens takes on this issue armed with an impressive alignment of survey data and legislative votes across an impressive range of issues including foreign policy, social welfare, economic policy, and religious issues (2012: 101).

Gilens' findings are sobering for anyone who hopes that the presence of formal democratic institutions guarantees that policy will be responsive even to the "median voter," much less the full range of public opinion. Instead, he finds a "complete lack of government responsiveness to the preferences of the poor [that] is disturbing and seems consistent only with the most cynical views of American politics" (2012: 81). This lack of influence extends to the preferences of a large swathe of the electorate, suggesting that legislative responsiveness is often restricted to those who are most advantaged, consistent with the "power elite" models of the political system that will be discussed in the next chapter. There is some support for claims of democratic responsiveness, particularly in that policy proposals adopted close in time to elections tend to match public opinion more closely. Gilens also finds that gridlocked or divided governments do less, but what they do is more responsive to voter preferences as expressed through public opinion surveys (2012: 211).

Note, however, that Gilens starts with the assumption that all voters have preferences that can be linked to the policies actually under consideration by Congress; this is baked in by the methodology of public opinion surveys that form an important component of his data for analysis. Yet, if we recall John Gaventa's puzzlement over the "quiescence" of Appalachian miners despite their everyday experience of exploitation and oppression (chapter 1), preferences themselves are problematic. In a great many circumstances, people who "should" make demands – at least in the opinion of outside observers and experts – fail to make those claims on the political system and, in some cases, reject those claims when made for them (see chapter 5 on the Tea Party as policy feedback). Such failures to understand and advance one's self-interest seem desperately at odds with the assumptions of rational voter models. But they pose questions that have provoked important new lines of sociological research.

Just as research on revolution has turned to specific organizational settings or patterns of interaction as sources of mobilization, students of democratic politics have also come to see political behavior as emerging from modes of interaction and the accumulation of experience. At the individual level, the puzzle is how to explain how individuals come to understand their interests and to understand some problems – but not others – as targets of political action. For Nina Eliasoph (1997), this question emerged in the course of a political ethnography of civic associations in a suburban community. Her informants had mobilized in local groups to address the problem of drug abuse and sales, but seemed complacent when it came to the nuclear battleships that cruised past their living room windows or the chemical spills in a nearby port. Why, Eliasoph wondered, were drugs "close to home" and therefore an accepted target for civic mobilization while battleships and industrial pollution were not?

Eliasoph's explanation begins with the recognition of a kind of cultural rule, the expectation that within a democratic system the exercise of citizenship should be consequential. Because of this, her subjects gravitated to issues where they hoped that they could make a difference: "the *goal* was to *feel* empowered; they had to forget that there were wide arenas in which they did feel powerless" (1997: 612). Recalling John Gaventa's typology of levels of power (chapter 1), the insight here is that there is a cultural space between accepting a potentially troublesome situation as natural or taken-for-granted and mobilizing around grievances. Problems may be recognized but bracketed as not "close to home." In this way, the failure to pay attention to an issue can be recast as an individual choice: "volunteers were working hard to switch off their attention to the wider world in order to maintain a feeling of control and sovereignty in everyday citizenship" (1997: 620). This pattern did not stop at bracketing battleships and industrial toxins: "in Parent League meetings, volunteers actively avoided talking about the race problems in the high school, the lack of funds for library books, heating, music, and theater supplies, and other potentially troubling topics that newcomers tried to raise"

(1997: 623). If there was no prospect of making a difference, the etiquette of good citizenship that prevailed in this community required that problems and grievances remain unmentioned.

A particularly striking instance of the failure to translate grievances into political claims has been documented by Sandra Levitsky (2014) in her study of family caregivers. She asks why the emotionally and financially demanding experience of caring for ill family members has not fueled a demand for expanded public support. Through their sharing of experiences in support groups, caregivers come to formulate grievances and to recognize how existing policies provide models for possible solutions that would provide support for others in their often desperate situations. But the organizational landscape of social service provision and the deeply engrained belief in the primacy of a family's responsibility for its own members block the translation of those grievances into policy demands and political preferences. Even though many of these caregivers come to articulate what they need from government, they are not then mobilized as citizens to demand what they want for themselves and for those for whom they care.

Yet powerlessness is not inevitable. As other research has demonstrated, those who are excluded from the polity may find new organizational forms that make it possible to translate social closure into effective voice (Clemens 1997; Young 2006). Government programs and agencies can be reorganized in ways that make it possible to see more directly how participation can shape outcomes, thereby setting in train virtuous cycles that actively and repeatedly engage citizens in their own government (Sirianni 2014). Public schools or great state universities anchor a sense of membership in support for public programs; policies of school choice and privatization may be implemented in ways that "individualize" public goods or require citizens to make significant contributions through higher tuition fees, transforming what had been perceived as a "public good" into a private choice about consumption. Therefore to understand these political paradoxes, when fully enfranchised democratic citizens articulate grievances and interests and yet do not act politically, it is necessary to turn from the level of individual action to think about political systems and policy regimes. To act politically often requires not just wanting something but also feeling that it is a legitimate, just, widely shared, and possible goal to achieve. Those horizons of possibility, the sense of what can be desired and what can be envisioned as possible, have powerful effects in shaping the distribution of rational apathy. In these ways, existing institutional arrangements and public policy may generate either their own support or pressures that fuel mobilization for political change.

5
Bringing the State Back In

At the center of political sociology, there is a recurring chicken-and-egg question. Should explanations begin with the action of individuals and the structural bases of social groups as causes of political outcomes? Or is it more compelling to begin with state structures and policies in order to account for the preferences and behavior of individuals? As with all good chicken-and-egg questions, in the end there is no decisive answer. But if the last chapter reviewed arguments that move from individuals in society to the state and public policy, this chapter surveys important arguments that take the opposite perspective.

These arguments reinforce one of the important findings of research on revolution (chapter 3): the form of political order at one time shapes the possibilities for politics going forward. Thus to understand why a democratic majority supports one party or policy rather than another, it is not enough to trace their decisions back to their membership in social groups or biographical sets of cultural and religious influences. Instead, the political decisions made by individuals are strongly shaped by the options that are available within the political system, the number of opportunities for mobilization or for vetoing proposals, and the perceived costs and benefits of state intervention. All this shaping, in turn, depends on the degree to which state officials act and state policies are determined in ways that are at least partially independent of the influence of mobilized social groups and mass opinion.

This theoretical turn in political sociology built in important ways on the great interest in early modern state formation and revolution that blossomed in the 1960s through the 1980s (chapters 2 and 3). If states – and the overthrow of states – were fascinating and consequential for the understanding of political history, surely a similar focus could reveal important aspects of contemporary politics. In order to generate such insights, however, it was necessary first to "bring the state back in" to political sociology and then to develop a new conceptual vocabulary and analytic toolkit to refurbish a concept that had long been out of intellectual fashion.

Bringing the State Back In

As we learned in the previous chapter, research on the social determinants of voting and the activities of civic associations dominated much of mid-twentieth-century political sociology. Individual voters and interest groups were assumed to be the "inputs" of a political system that would be influenced by these factors and, in time, produce "outputs" in the form of public policies and public services (Skocpol 1985: 4; see also Mitchell 1991: 78–81). Often linked to the "behavioral turn" in political science, these arguments aligned with the image of the individual voter as a carrier of attributes and preferences which, in turn, might be understood as aspects of that individual's socio-economic location. Attention turned away from the durable configurations of social networks and political ordering that are central to contemporary political sociology.

Within postwar political sociology, however, there was an important counter to this focus on electoral democracy. C. Wright Mills (1916–62) captured the core of the argument in the title of one of his most influential books, *The Power Elite* (1956). Mills' core claim was that networks of institutional elites – from government, business, the military, and the most prestigious universities and foundations –

determined government policy. Some proponents of this line of analysis linked it to broadly Marxist claims about the influence of business leaders – or "capital" more generally – over political decisions, although similar arguments could be grounded in a lineage of work on status orders and elite formation within American sociology. In the first edition of his widely reprinted and multiply updated *Who Rules America* (1967: 1), G. William Domhoff located his analysis at the conjuncture of Mills' argument with studies by Digby Baltzell (1915–96) of the "American business aristocracy" and Marxian concepts of the "ruling class." Domhoff sought to demonstrate that evidence of pluralism in local politics was "not incompatible with the idea of a national upper class that is a governing class." To make such an argument required demonstration of network structure within social and economic elites, as well as significant ties between those elites and the holders of political power. By the time of the fifth edition in 2005, this becomes a theory of "class dominance." Domhoff uses evidence of connections between corporate elites and political actors to support claims for business influence over public policy (for an extended illustration of this approach to the interpretation of the policies adopted under the New Deal of Franklin Delano Roosevelt, see Domhoff 1996). Such arguments presented the relation between business and the state as predominantly instrumental, allocating the agency and intentions that mattered to business.

While the analyses of elite power countered assumptions about the influence of democratic electorates, they still located much of the force of their analysis outside of formal governmental institutions and left "the state" as a kind of black box. By the late 1960s and early 1970s, a wide range of scholars began to attend to this gap in political and social theory, asserting that "the state" was an important but poorly understood concept in sociology (Abrams 1988 [1977]; Nettl 1968). The legacies of Karl Marx and Max Weber were particularly important in shaping these debates. For Marx, particularly in "The Eighteenth Brumaire," his essay on the Revolution of 1848 (see the discussions of work by Roger Gould and Mark Traugott in chapter 3), "the state" is presented as an instrumentality of whichever class rules at a given place and time. Thus the "absolutist" state gives way during revolution to the "bourgeois" state, which functions as an "executive committee" of the new ruling class in capitalist society. This approach led scholars to identify neo-Marxist approaches to the state as "instrumentalist" for their focus on how control of the state apparatus advanced the interests of particular classes or class fractions or how relatively autonomous state officials "do for capital what capital cannot do for itself" (Skocpol 1980). Such theories clearly had strong affinities with models of the power elite.

The incorporation of Weberian influences, however, redirected attention toward the formal organization of state action and authority. Weber's enormously influential studies of bureaucracy informed a concept of the state as an administrative structure, which could be characterized by variations in the level of professionalization, rationalization, and other dimensions rather than the identity of the class actors in control. The cluster of concepts that highlight the training and qualification of state officials as well as the formal features of law support a model of politics in which agency shifts from socio-economic groups in civil society to office-holders and technocrats. As Theda Skocpol argued in her influential essay "Bringing the State Back In" (1985: 9): "States conceived as organizations claiming control over territories and people may formulate and pursue goals that are not simply reflective of the demands or interests of social groups, classes, or society ... Unless such independent goal formulation occurs, there is little need to talk about states as important actors."

For this vision of the state, new analytics were required. As a first step, scholars offered new conceptual definitions such as J. P. Nettl's claim that the state can be understood as "a collectivity that summates a set of functions and structures in order to generalize their applicability" (1968: 562). Notice what has shifted from the definition of the state offered by Weber as an organization with a "monopoly on legitimate violence within a territory" (see chapter 1). In Nettl's conceptualization, states are not associated solely with coercion and domination but also with the embodiment of a quality of general membership that points toward the cultural constructs of belonging that are central to discussions of nationalism (chapter 2). But, like the original Weberian inspiration, this line of argument emphasized that "the state" represented an actor or potentiality that could not be reduced to the expression of some underlying configuration of class alliances.

Variations in State Autonomy and State Capacity

A focus solely on state autonomy invites the same kind of disappearance of the social that marks the foundations of liberal democracy in contract theory. The temptation is to think of the state as a single, bounded actor that "possesses" a particular degree of strength or portfolio of resources that "it" uses to exercise domination over its subjects. Here is the point where it is important to reach back to the basic concepts of power introduced in chapter 1, remembering that power is both embedded in systems of relationships and exercised through those relationships. States do not have effects in vacuums, but rather through multiple kinds of social networks. As Skocpol signaled with the inauguration of this political project: "Bringing the state back in to a central place in analyses of policy making and social change does require a break with some of the most encompassing social-determinist assumptions of pluralism, structure-functionalist developmentalism, and the various neo-Marxisms. But it does not mean that old theoretical emphases should simply be turned on their heads" (1985: 20).

This insight led Peter Evans (1995) to formulate the important concept of "embedded autonomy." Although the term seems to embody a contradiction, Evans used it to capture the ways in which the capacity of state officials and agencies to make things happen depended in large part on the quantity and quality of their relations with other social actors. Here, a kind of Goldilocks principle prevailed – if state officials were too isolated from social actors, they lacked leverage, but if they were too tightly connected, state efforts would be "captured" by the interests of non-state actors.

Given Evans' research on countries outside of the Weberian heartland of Western Europe, he has been particularly concerned about the conditions under which a degree of state autonomy emerges in societies that have long been governed through networks based on patronage and kinship (see chapter 2). Reflecting on the culture of complaint about the inefficiency and corruption of state agencies, he reminds us that:

> the state lies at the center of solutions to the problem of order. Without the state, markets, the other master institution of modern society, cannot function. We do not spend our valuable time standing in lines in front of the counters of bureaucrats because we are masochists. We stand there because we need what the state provides. We need predictable rules, and these in turn must have a concrete organizational structure behind them. We need some organizational reflection, however imperfect, of general as opposed to individual interests. We need something beyond caveat emptor to sustain the process of exchange. We need "collective goods" like sewage systems, roads, and schools. (Evans 1995: 1–2)

In this passage, Evans echoes familiar Weberian claims about how the state provides a framework of predictable law, reliable media of exchange, mechanisms for managing relations between members and strangers, and legitimate settlement of disputes over agreements and formal contracts (Collins 1980). Variation in these capacities produces different trajectories of economic development. Overly strong or "predatory" states can stifle growth (Chibber 2003), while insufficiently strong states fail to provide the institutional frameworks necessary for the development of markets and the trust, predictability, and standardization on which they depend. In a quantitative cross-national study, Evans and Rauch (1999) demonstrate the positive effect of two elements of "Weberianness" – meritocratic recruitment of state officials and the existence of a predictable career ladder for those officials – on economic growth. To the extent that the stability and capacity of a state structure depend on "performance legitimacy" (Zhao 2009) or delivering benefits to citizens, the capacity to generate economic growth feeds back into greater support for state officials and their policies.

But Evans' core concept is "embedded autonomy" not "state autonomy." In his analysis, "embedded" points to the importance of the relations – whether of control, collaboration, or dependence – between state agencies and other social actors. State agencies can seed and support new enterprises, they can focus on regulation, or they can even directly create and control government-owned firms across a range of industries. If fascist regimes (chapter 3) accumulate power by absorbing the capacities of as many social networks and organizations as possible, Evans' study of state-led economic development strategies in Brazil, India, and South Korea underscored the dynamic quality of state–society relations: "Successful transformation changes the nature of the state's private counterparts, making effective future state involvement dependent on the reconstruction of state–society ties" (1995: 17). Reconstruction in a way that leads to the "capture" of state agencies by private actors can be economically damaging as well as politically exclusionary. But, Evans asserts, "expanding the scope of state–society links to include a broader range of groups and classes, however difficult that might be to accomplish, should result in a more politically robust and adaptive version of embedded autonomy" (1995: 228).

Notice how this analysis resonates with the imagery of states emerging within social cages constructed through linkages across different types of social networks (chapter 1). Evans emphasizes the importance both of the expansiveness of those interconnections and the moderated balance of power within such relations. As Skocpol underlines, "the very *structural potentials* for autonomous state actions change over time, as the organizations of coercion and administration undergo transformations, both internally and in their relations to societal groups and to representative parts of government" (1985: 14; original emphasis). Thus it follows that the degree and support for state autonomy can only be understood by putting state structures in relationship to other circuits and social networks, a claim that resonates with earlier accounts of political ordering embedded in systems of social ties.

This project has led some scholars and theorists away from a predominantly Weberian account that starts from an understanding of power as the capacity of one actor to influence the actions of another against his or her will, just as

Gaventa pointed to additional dimensions of power that might exclude some individuals or issues from political considerations or to the state's influence in the shaping of the identities and preferences that are expressed through political action (Orloff 2012). Here, as in studies of early modern state formation (chapter 3), the work of Michel Foucault has provided important theoretical resources. By focusing on flows of power, particularly in its "capillary" or most extended forms in the designs of everyday institutions such as schools and prisons or practices of self-regulation, the scope of state influence is recognized as extended well beyond the boundaries of formal political institutions, the agencies so often imagined as housed in great white marble buildings. This approach reframes cases that might have been described as characterized by "low Weberianness" (Evans and Rauch 1999) as societies "in which those modern techniques that make the state appear to be a separate entity that somehow stands outside society had not yet been institutionalized" (Mitchell 1991: 91). If, as Timothy Mitchell has argued, we should understand the distinction between state and society "not as the boundary between two discrete entities, but as a line drawn internally within the network of institutional mechanisms through which a social and political order is maintained" (1991: 78), even the presence of a large cluster of such white marble buildings should not trick us into thinking that "the state is *there*" as a bounded organizational actor. State structures, as with almost all conceivable orderings of political power, operate through, and in turn transform, the ordering of surrounding networks of social relationships and practices.

At the most basic level, states may literally remake their worlds. A flight over the Great Plains on a clear day reveals one method of parceling out land and building roads that has had durable environmental effects; the hedgerows evident in parts of Europe testify to other approaches. Some of the most durable marks of the state upon landscapes reflect efforts to transform territory into a set of resources that can be counted, extracted, and deployed. James C. Scott, in *Seeing Like a State* (1998), captures this effect in a discussion of the "fiscal forestry" practices by the nineteenth-century Prussian state in what is now Germany. In this system of governing nature, "the actual tree with its vast number of possible uses was replaced by an abstract tree representing a volume of lumber or firewood." From this vantage point, much was missed: "all those trees, bushes, and plants holding little or no potential for state revenue ... all those parts of trees, even revenue-bearing trees, which might have been useful to the population but whose value could not be converted into fiscal receipts" (1998: 12). As practiced by increasingly professionalized state foresters, this vision of the forests resulted in a "great simplification of the forest into a 'one-commodity machine' ... [that] severely bracketed, or assumed to be constant, all variables except those bearing directly on the yield of the selected species and on the cost of growing and extracting them" (1998: 20). In the short term, the approach was gratifyingly successful, leading to increased timber harvest; with the next rotation of trees in a scientifically managed forest, the limitations appeared in the form of what came to be known as *Waldsterben* or "forest death." The enormously complex web of forest ecology had been deeply damaged by being rearranged in terms that maximized the fiscal interests of the state.

Scott's argument focuses on the damage caused by the "high modernist" state through its insistence on simplifying and rationalizing complex, organic systems whether of natural environments or social systems. Transposed to political sociology, this model of state effects on the social has been incorporated to understand how "policy makes politics" and shapes the trajectories of state development stretching over decades and even centuries: "As defined by Theda Skocpol, 'policy feedback' refers to the ways 'policies, once enacted, restructure subsequent political processes.' Skocpol pointed to two kinds of feedback effects: New policies may transform state capacities by creating, building upon, or undercutting administrative arrangements; and they may affect the identities, political goals, and capabilities of social groups" (Mettler and Soss 2004: 60). In this second way, the recognition of feedback effects is one approach for rediscovering the social relations and networks within democratic politics.

Policy Feedbacks on Perceptions of Self-Interest and Grievances

The influence of the modern state is not limited to the actions of state bureaucrats and elected officials or the ways in which they use official positions in order to gain advantage with respect to mobilized citizens or opposing factions. The consequences of policies also shape the ways in which individual citizens come to understand their interests, hopes, and grievances as well as the paths they take – or do not take – to advance their claims.

A striking example of this can be found in the political behavior of senior citizens in the United States. As we learned in chapter 4, rates of political participation tend to increase with both income and education. But citizens over 65 provide a puzzling exception to this pattern. The puzzle is specifically in the lower half of the distribution of economic and educational advantages; poorer and less-educated seniors vote at higher levels than comparable non-seniors with similar levels of schooling and similar incomes (Campbell 2003: 26, 59). To explain this pattern, Andrea Campbell points to the unusual features of Social Security, the federal system of old age insurance which is supported by a payroll tax on earned income. Social Security is "distinctive in what it means for politics in the United States. It mobilizes a low-income group around an economic issue; Social Security has participatory effects on all seniors, boosting their activity levels, but these are greatest for low-income seniors" (2003: 40). Whereas evidence of the minimal impact of public opinion of the non-wealthy may produce the kind of "rational apathy" discussed in chapter 4 (see Gilens 2012), senior citizens are keenly aware of the direct benefit embodied in a monthly Social Security check, an "earned benefit" to which they contributed throughout their working lives. Although this phrasing misrepresents the actual financing of Social Security by taxation of current workers to support current retirees (rather than the earlier payroll taxes of those now-retirees locked up in an imagined savings account), it sustains an often fierce attachment to the program and a potential for rapid and punishing political mobilization against any politician who would suggest limiting its benefits.

Campbell directly contrasts the unusual power of Social Security to mobilize those with low incomes to the movement for property tax rollbacks that succeeded in the adoption of Proposition 13 in California in 1978, attributing this mobilization to "the large tax savings the measure promised" its supporters (2003: 40). In *The Permanent Tax Revolt*, however, Isaac Martin (2008) demonstrates that this mobilization cannot be explained solely by looking at the economic effects of policies such as the level of the property tax. Although tax revolts are perceived retrospectively as a conservative project, Martin argued that they are better understood as a response to state-building and modernization, which can be expressed in the language of either the political right or left. California was an exemplar of how market-driven increases in real estate prices shifted individuals' exposure to taxation. Without doing anything but failing to move, a taxpayer could find themselves with a greatly increased property tax bill. This effect intensified as technocrats in the state tax authority introduced methods for tracking fluctuations in real estate pricing much more closely. Rather than waiting until a house is resold to change its value and recalculate the tax bill, state agencies recalculated what was owed in property taxes with every shift in the real estate market. In this telling, anti-tax mobilization is often a response to "modernizing" tax reforms that result in greater rationalization or consistency and thereby eliminate the informal protections of partial, out-dated assessments.

Policy feedback models, therefore, offer an important contrast to the classic sociological model of voting (chapter 4) in which values and interests were presumed to be "read off" of socio-economic location. Linked to the recognition of degrees of state autonomy in policy decisions, this perspective underscores how political outcomes can reshape patterns of social behavior and distributions of preferences and belief. Sometimes, as in the case of senior citizens, policy design can intensify political participation. Other policies, implemented in different ways, can have the opposite effect as Cybelle Fox (2012) traces in her study of the administration of relief and social welfare in the early New Deal. For

European immigrants, these services provided not only relief but a pathway that encouraged them to achieve citizenship. Mexicans and Mexican Americans, by contrast, received far less generous relief based on presumptions that they not only lacked work but lacked the will to work. Relief organizations were much less likely to encourage naturalization for Mexicans and became part of a policy machinery that organized many (including some Mexican Americans with US citizenship) across the border and out of the polity altogether.

Just as Peter Evans (1995) underscored the dynamic quality of state–society relations when it comes to fostering trajectories of economic development, policy feedback models highlight the ways in which political changes and new policies may have lasting impacts on patterns of political mobilization. State policies shape preferences, the probability that citizens will act on preferences, and the likelihood that citizens will understand government as either the source of their problems or as a possible solution. In the United States, the rapid rise of the Tea Party movement provides only the most recent and compelling example of this phenomenon.

The Puzzle of the Tea Party

Over the past few decades, electoral politics in the United States have provided rich material for thinking through the relationship of classic sociological models of voting to the claims of policy feedback theories. Recall that the sociological model of voting begins with the individual located in "social structures, social context, social networks, and processes of social communication and influence" (Mettler and Soss 2004: 57). In its economic variant, those locations are the basis for rational understandings of self-interest which, in turn, should inform opinion on policy and voting decisions. Given this theoretical starting point, one of the most startling features of recent American presidential elections is that large portions of the working and middle class vote for Republican candidates even as the Republican Party tends to advance policies that are geared to the economic interests of the wealthy. Why, scholars and pundits ask, would those who are likely to benefit from increased government spending be inclined to vote for the party committed to lowering tax rates for the wealthy and cutting government programs?

One of the most influential early answers to this question was provided by the essayist Thomas Frank in *What's the Matter with Kansas?* (2004), who described a "derangement" prevalent in his home state of Kansas. Recounting the political biography of a friend's father who had gone from voting for the liberal Democrat George McGovern for President to supporting "the farthest-right Republicans he can find on the ballot," Frank continues to tell us that this man had come to agree with politicians and pundits who denounced the teachers' unions to which he had belonged during his working life. A similar pattern, Frank argued, was evident at the level of their town: "Even as Republican economic policy laid waste to the city's industries, unions, and neighborhoods, the townsfolk responded by lashing out on cultural issues, eventually winding up with a hard-right Republican congressman, a born-again Christian who campaigned largely on an anti-abortion platform. Today the city looks like a miniature Detroit" (Frank 2004: 4–5). The language of "derangement," backlash, and "cultural anger" suggests that the explanation lies in a stirring up of irrational passions that prevent voters from understanding their genuine interests grounded in their socio-economic situations.

Studies of policy feedback provide an alternative explanation. In a clever set of survey experiments, Suzanne Mettler (2011) revealed a key process of misrecognizing government benefits. An early question in her survey asked simply whether the respondent had "ever used a government social program." Fifty-seven percent said they had not. The follow-up asked about a set of 21 specific programs "including Social Security, unemployment insurance, the home-mortgage-interest deduction and student loans. It turned out that 94 percent of those who had denied using programs had benefited from at least one; the average respondent had used four." And there was a distinctive pattern to government programs that were not initially recognized as government programs; they were more likely to benefit those who were better off, more likely to be administered through tax deductions such as that for home mortgage interest and for private employers who provide health insurance for their employees, or more likely to be perceived as "earned," with Social Security as the prime example of this type.

This misrecognition provides the basis for a revision of Thomas Frank's account for *What's the Matter with Kansas?* Rather than explaining lower-middle and working-class support for Republican candidates as the product of a distraction or mystification by cultural appeals, an analysis in terms of policy feedbacks highlights how voters understand the relationship between their contributions in the form of taxes and the distribution of benefits through public programs. Because so many government expenditures are obscured through complex systems of contracting-out and tax expenditures, direct support in the form of welfare checks or food stamps is often misrecognized as accounting for the vast majority of government spending.

The consequences of this selective recognition of government benefits became particularly visible in the Tea Party movement of conservatives that erupted during President Obama's first term in the wake of the financial crisis of 2008. While Tea Partiers famously waved signs demanding "Keep Government Out of My Medicare," they also formulated grievances not only against minorities and immigrants who were assumed to depend on government benefits but against their own younger relatives. "A lot of [young] people ... They just feel like they are entitled," explained one woman who went on to describe a nephew who had "been on welfare his whole life." Another man worried that "My grandson, he's fourteen and he asked me: 'Why should I work, why can't I just get free money?'" The worry was that "young people are being taught that they deserve support from the government." College students were the target of similar criticisms from one Congressman who declared that "you can go to school, collect your Pell Grants, get food stamps, low-income energy assistance, section 8 housing, and all of a sudden we find ourselves subsidizing people that don't have to graduate from college" (Skocpol and Williamson 2012: 72–3). Thus the variation in the recognition of government-funded benefits *as* government benefits drove lines of criticism and conflict through family networks as well as between those of different races and in greatly varying economic circumstances.

Policy Feedbacks and Party Politics

If analyses of the Tea Party and the rightward turn in American electoral politics illuminate how policy feedbacks shape individual preferences and participation, similar effects can also be documented at the level of policy regimes and national governments. Recall that a part of the ideological framework for liberal democracy is that individuals, through an imagined "social contract," give up their natural rights to a sovereign power in return for security. As the understanding of "security" has expanded beyond protection from brute force, the failure of states to deliver social provision – or the failure of citizens to perceive that they are being helped by their government – can unravel the basic bargain that legitimates the existing order. What kind of politics follows from this failure?

Policy feedback arguments trace a loop from government programs back through the preferences of individual voters. But in many cases, the answer to "what is my government doing for me?" is not enough to mobilize voters and shape the electorate. Beyond policy impacts, party organizations play a central role in shaping which dimensions of identity and what ways of assessing government activity are actually influential in motivating political participation and shaping the preferences of citizens. As de Leon et al. (2015) argue, parties do not simply reflect or respond to some given distribution of voter traits or preferences. Instead, much of what parties do is to "articulate" social divisions and similarities with the political system. This analysis provides a powerful counter to sociological arguments that present politics as a reflection of social ties and identities. Parties, in this analysis, actively articulate identities, cleavages, and interests that sustain and are sustained by the governments they make. If, as the earlier discussion of the sociological model of voting made clear (chapter 4), there is no reliably strong association between socio-economic location and voting choices, this may be in part due to an absence of party efforts to articulate political loyalties in class terms.

A powerful illustration of this dynamic is provided by Mabel Berezin (2009) in a comparative study of the rightward turn in French and Italian politics in the late twentieth century. Her theoretical contribution to this debate is to insist on the importance of the cultural dimensions of politics, specifically the ways in which *nation-states* represent consequential configurations of identity and security. So whereas many commentators have pointed to the rise of xenophobia and new kinds of ethnic politics in Europe as driven primarily by individual values and identities, she argues that they are better interpreted as a response to the diminishing ability or willingness of many European states to provide basic security, particularly in economic and social terms. Rather than focusing on immigration as an economic threat to individuals or a trigger for deep-seated forms of prejudice, Berezin reminds us that much of the heightened fear of immigration (particularly from Eastern Europe as personified by the "Polish plumber") is a product of the expansion of the European Union with its concomitant undercutting of national regimes of social provision and sources of sovereignty. As leaders of center parties ceased to articulate political loyalties in terms of core programs of social provision, parts of the French electorate drifted away from familiar ways of understanding their political selves. Although some French voters possessed "thick" identity-based loyalties to the right-wing National Front (NF) party, others voted for or approved of the NF as one of the few options for expressing deep-seated concerns about the erosion of the expectations of social security that had been established during France's post-war development as a centralized welfare state. Exposure to increasingly volatile markets sets in train a deep unraveling of the foundations of political order.

The repeated findings that policy design has significant effects on political behavior and "rational apathy" have not been lost on practical politicians. The ascendance of conservative politics in both Britain and the United States in the 1980s was accompanied by efforts to replace direct and universal forms of social provision with programs that rested on privatization and choice, thereby eroding the power of shared policy interests to mobilize broad categories of voters (Hacker and Pierson 2005; Pierson 1994). This approach illuminates how policy design expresses political strategy as well as technocratic projects of implementation. Campbell's study of political participation by senior citizens makes this point with respect to proposals for the privatization of this key element of the American welfare state:

> Reform has significant implications for democratic citizenship, altering both Social Security's political engagement and its resource effects. Individual management of Social Security assets could break the tie between senior citizens and their government. Seniors would be less interested in what the government does, since the government would be responsible for a smaller portion of their retirement income. This cognitive link, this interest in public affairs that animates senior participation, would be diminished. The break would be most abrupt for low-income seniors, whose well-being is so closely tied to government action. (Campbell 2003: 143)

Here, processes of policy feedback have the potential to produce the same patterns of "rational apathy" that have been traced to interaction etiquettes in civil society and perceptions of political impotence on the part of voters (chapter 4). To the extent that participation responds to the provision of benefits, minimizing those benefits or making them harder to understand is another method of "structuring the electorate." Because policy makes politics, the decreased generosity and visibility of public benefits can also undermine the social bases for political participation. But where policy itself leaves open questions of how rules will be implemented and enforced, the result may be to elicit engagement by those potentially covered by a new law as they seek to define for themselves the terms of its enforcement (Edelman et al. 1999).

Policy Feedback and the Organizational State

Policy can provide motives – or not – for political participation, but it can also contribute to the capacity for political organization. This dynamic is particularly pronounced when governments rely on private or party organizations to carry out important political functions ranging from the mobilization of voters to the delivery of publicly funded services. A striking example of these dynamics can be found in a close study of the relationships among elected officials, nonprofit organizations, and communities in Brooklyn, one of the boroughs that make up New York City. Rejecting the dominant tendency to equate organization solely with membership and sociability, Nicole Marwell (2007) argues that formal organizations are not simply sites for the formation of social capital (see chapter 4), but also vehicles for projects that accumulate resources and potentially expand opportunities and political networks within poor communities. Organizational efforts are crucial to securing the external resources necessary to provide opportunities for housing, political influence, and employment. They also make visible – and mobilize – the relationship between benefits and participation.

The significance of such efforts is plain in the neighborhoods that Marwell studied, communities that had been undercut by "growth machine" projects and road construction plans that directed activity to the suburbs, exacerbating the effects of de-industrialization and urban decay. Championed by local elites – real estate developers, bankers, car dealers, and others who benefited from growth – these policy-driven changes in the organization of urban life concentrated urban problems in specific neighborhoods while directing benefits elsewhere (Molotch 1976). In response, the 1960s and 1970s brought grassroots efforts to support housing rehabilitation, policing of open-air drug markets, and other local projects had contributed to a growing number of social service and nonprofit organizations. Initially, these organizations reestablished relationships with city government, particularly around the improvement (or, at least, slowed deterioration) of housing stock. But because these programs depended on federal funding as well as local voluntarism, these community-based organizations emerged as key nodes articulating local and national politics, public policy and economic development. Nonprofit organizations became sites for the mobilization of gratitude and electoral support for politicians who had secured government resources for the community. These capacities for community-centered mobilization took on greater importance as investors and developers rediscovered these long-neglected neighborhoods as New York City enjoyed a glittering resurgence by the 1990s. Somewhat ironically, the organizations that were born in a response to urban decay became eventual partners in the revival and even gentrification of those communities.

Such ties of financial dependence and political alliance can also be sources of vulnerability for civic organizations. As Michael McQuarrie (2013) recounts in a study of urban development efforts in the city of Cleveland, the very processes that secured the organizational stability of community development organizations also undercut their capacity to serve as vehicles for political action as opposed to mechanisms for securing the passive assent of the governed and legitimation of the authority of civic elites who had not been elected to office. These relationships, through which community activists became tied to financial elites, helps to explain how a city with an extraordinarily rich endowment of civic organizations – both community-based and elite – proved so overwhelmed in the face of the housing crisis that undercut the core premises of the city's template for doing politics and economic development.

These two examples from the intersection of urban sociology and political sociology illuminate the politics that become visible when we understand the distinction between state and society "not as the boundary between two discrete entities, but as a line drawn internally within the network of institutional mechanisms through which a social and political order is maintained" (Mitchell 1991: 78). But where each of these cases centers on a shift in political balance – the ascendance of nonprofit organizations as powerful political brokers in Brooklyn as compared to their impotence in the face of crisis in Cleveland – other research has pointed to still broader feedback effects to explain the persistence of distinctive regimes of social provision established across the advanced industrial democracies.

Politics Makes Policy Makes Politics: The Sociology of the Welfare State

Stepping back to consider the forces that produce broad combinations of policies in different countries, scholars have focused on how successful political efforts set reinforcing dynamics into motion. For scholars of the welfare state, one of the central questions has turned on the seemingly "laggard" and "underdeveloped" character of the American welfare state. Until the reforms of the New Deal in the 1930s, which established Social Security for the aged among other major programs, the American welfare state had consisted largely of state-level supports for mothers and children and a collection of programs related to injuries on the job that could deprive a family of their primary breadwinner. These observations provoked new lines of historical research which, in turn, demonstrated that the "absences" of the American welfare state (notably a national system of health insurance) accompanied a set of unusually early developments in the support of public education as well as family and old age support through a system of military pensions for veterans of the Civil War. For organizations of those veterans, above all, the legislative victories securing and funding those pensions produced more support and larger membership in those organizations, setting in train a dynamic in which veterans' benefits would be among the most generous sources of tax-supported social provision for decades to come (Mettler 2005; Skocpol 1992).

These arguments aligned with an increasingly configurational approach to the study of the welfare state. Rather than conceptualizing welfare regimes as simply "strong" or "weak," what was important was to notice that the policy pieces tended to fit together in a limited number of patterns. For many scholars, the key variations involved relationships among government, industry, and workers in the organization of the economy. Described in terms of corporatism or "varieties of capitalism," these analyses demonstrated how patterns of alliance and collaboration – or their absence – influenced the level and volatility of unemployment, the acquisition of skill by workers, and the possibilities of retraining as an adaptation to economic change (Hall and Soskice 2001).

Gøsta Esping-Andersen captured a different version of this insight in his analysis of "worlds of welfare," arguing that welfare regimes in the advanced industrial democracies could be sorted into three categories: "liberal" welfare states that combine "means-tested assistance, modest universal transfers, or modest social-insurance plans"; "corporatist" regimes in which benefits are attached to status (e.g. blue-collar, white-collar) and oriented to the preservation of traditional family forms"; and "social democratic" welfare states in which rights and benefits are extended to the middle as well as working class in alignment with commitments to universalism (1990: 26–7). In explaining why different nation-states developed different kinds of welfare states, he drew on familiar theoretical resources, particularly the "class-coalition" thesis from Barrington Moore's influential analysis of what led countries to take the diverging paths to dictatorship and democracy (chapter 3). From this perspective, the unusually comprehensive and egalitarian version of welfare state exemplified by a country such as Sweden can be attributed to "the capacity of (variably) strong working-class movements to forge a political alliance with farmer organizations" (1990: 18) as these alliances played out in the existing institutional framework for politics. In a warning to those who might seek a simpler account for the variations in scope or generosity of such policy regimes, Esping-Andersen warned that "the hope of finding one single powerful causal force must be abandoned; the task is to identify salient interaction-effects," particularly those among patterns of class mobilization, class-political coalition structures, and the institutional history of different regimes (1990: 29).

In making family central to his analysis of welfare regimes, Esping-Andersen drew upon a rich literature by feminist scholars interested in the ways in which public policy perpetuated or potentially eradicated systems of gender inequality (Fraser 1990; Pateman 1998; Ruggie 1984; for a review of this research agenda, see Orloff 2009). As with the "multiple networks" approach to the study of political orders (Mann 1986), this feminist scholarship focused on the ways in which social policy supported distinctive family forms that were, in turn, entwined with distinctive ways of organizing labor markets. Thus the shape of any particular welfare regime was constituted out of an intersection – and at times a highly contested intersection – of multiple divisions of labor and coalition structures. As a consequence, the politics of welfare states cannot be read from any single perspective. In particular, "decommodification" or minimizing the dependence of citizens on the labor market to secure their well-being, may appear as a benefit to those already in the labor market but a further obstacle to those defined by different relations of dependence, particularly on the family (Orloff 1993).

Much of the comparative literature on welfare states takes this historical or genealogical approach, tracing the sources of variation to the differences in the configuration of class alliances or sequences of enfranchisement, bureaucratization, and industrialization that should be familiar from the earlier discussions of democratization (chapter 3). Yet, once set in motion, these historical origins may constitute durable feedbacks (Lee 2012), reshaping patterns of social organization in ways that may support either the reproduction of distinctive policy approaches (as illustrated by the durable generosity of veterans' benefits in the United States) or their destabilization (Lee et al. 2011).

Institutional Analysis in Political Sociology

In demonstrating how configurations of political order shape trajectories of change, these broadly "institutionalist" literatures converge on an important metatheoretical point. Whereas liberal contract theory – along with much of post-war social science – starts from the assumptions of "methodological individualism," in which order is understood as the aggregation of individual behavior and decisions, institutional approaches highlight how social context and relatively durable configurations of social order shape the possibilities for action. To return again to the insight offered by Michel Crozier, "the pattern of change, and not the amount of change itself, must be considered as the basic variable" (1964: 226).

This claim holds for the pattern of reproduction and the reliable reconstruction of the features that are most distinctive to one polity or another (Clemens and Cook 1999). Conflicts over seemingly identical issues may take substantially different forms as actors draw on different cultural discourses and seek to take advantage of varying opportunities in the judicial or legislative systems (Ferree et al. 2002). Policy feedback models exemplify institutional accounts of reproduction as current public programs construct voter preferences and patterns of participation that produce pressure for the continuation of those same programs. Different configurations of policy may minimize pressure for their continuation, allowing for a pattern of change through restriction of government benefits. In many circumstances, however, institutional effects may generate grievances alongside pressures for reproduction. In such cases, the first question raised involves the balance of forces among those who are advantaged and those who might come to see their disadvantage as a reason to mobilize for change. The second question turns on when and how such mobilization for change occurs – and when it makes change happen.

6
Social Movements and Social Change

Social stability is easily taken for granted. The way that the world was yesterday very often provides us with an accurate prediction of the way it will be tomorrow. But this piece of common sense leads us into a theoretical trap when it comes to understanding processes of social and political change. In order to understand how transformations are possible, it is necessary to start by highlighting the processes that maintain the already existing order. Recall Michael Mann's foundational argument about the character of "social cages" (chapter 1). The emergence of systems of ordered power relations is made possible by the development of interdependence and the benefits that individuals receive by virtue of their role in some division of labor. Despite acts of oppression and an unequal share of the harvest, individuals may choose to remain as subordinate members of a community with a system of irrigated agriculture rather than heading off on their own into the wild. This basic insight is shared with concepts of a more developed state as an organized system of extraction and coercion (Tilly 1992), systems in which those who gain the most from the arrangements will also exercise their capacity to block changes, particularly those that might lead to some redistribution either between different elites or between elites and masses (Kroneberg and Wimmer 2012; Skocpol 1980). Given such arrays of power, linked to the creation of those landscapes of castles, forts and temples, what are the conditions and processes that produce social change?

At first glance, one obvious answer might be found in the emotions and interests of those who are disadvantaged within such arrangements: the field workers who are beaten, the peasants who are forced to surrender a significant portion of their harvest. Frantz Fanon's account of the anger and resentment stoked by relations of colonialism (chapter 2) evokes such a causal chain: nation-building "is facilitated by the existence of this mortar kneaded with blood and rage" (2004 [1961]: 51). But while "grievances" are an important element in processes of mobilization, sociological studies have demonstrated that they are rarely sufficient. Many people, across time and space, go through their lives angry and resentful without ever mobilizing to demand significant change.

The ascendance of social movement studies as a major subfield within political sociology owes its origins to precisely this insight. As John McCarthy and Mayer Zald argued in the influential article that established "resource mobilization" as an important theoretical perspective, the "most influential approaches to an understanding of social movement phenomena for American sociologists during the past decade ... have in common strong assumptions that shared grievances and generalized beliefs (loose ideologies) about the causes and possible means of reducing grievances are important preconditions for the emergence of a social movement in a collectivity" (1977: 1214). These assumptions had led to a basic prediction: the angrier the people, the more mobilization. This perspective leads us to expect that social movements – and, in their extreme form, revolutions – will develop among those who are most deprived, most oppressed, and most exploited. But, as we have already learned from the literature on revolution (chapter 3), this is often not the case. Revolutionary actors may be those in a position to defend traditional orders (Calhoun 1983) or who understand themselves to have something important to lose (Traugott 1980). Developing their argument in the mid-1970s, with the tumult of the anti-war movement and the New Left still seething, McCarthy and Zald asserted a very different starting claim "that there is always enough discontent in any society to supply the grass-roots support for a movement if the movement is effectively organized and has at its disposal the power and resources of some established elite group" (1977: 1215). From this perspective, movements were more likely to succeed when they could mobilize financial resources (from members or allies), when they controlled meeting spaces (such as churches or private homes), and when they could draw on pre-existing collective identities and networks of social ties for recruitment.

McCarthy and Zald's manifesto for a new approach to the study of social movements helped to create, by the 1990s, the dominant theoretical model. Under the label of "political process" theory, it combined multiple key claims: the rejection of grievance-driven or psychological models along with analytic attention to resource mobilization, political opportunities, and "framing" processes. Translated from the specific vocabulary of the subfield, these last three elements involved attention to the organizational resources available to a movement (which might include financing, material support, or linkages to existing social networks and associations), political opportunities such as institutionalized decision points, including elections or divisions among those in power, and the cultural resources as they are deployed by movement leaders to "frame" grievances in ways that resonate with broadly held beliefs about what is just or what would constitute a solution (McAdam 1982; McAdam et al. 1996; Snow et al. 1986). This approach located much of the explanation of mobilization in the *context* for action rather than inside actors' heads, but at the cost of producing a thin model of mobilization processes that highlighted the work of elites and movement leaders manipulating "frames."

The result of this theoretical intervention, combined with the recent experience of a great wave of mobilization, was an efflorescence of sociological research on social movements. Former movement insiders did some of the work, starting from their own experience to build rigorous analyses of Students for a Democratic Society (Gitlin 1980), the women's liberation movement (Freeman 1974), or the United Farm Workers (Ganz 2000). Others, of the cohort of scholars that followed, sought to understand the sources of the surge of mobilization that seemed to be fading in the United States by the late 1970s, just as liberation movements appeared in developing countries around the globe (chapter 3).

In these efforts, social movement scholars recapitulated many of the lines of argument that appeared elsewhere in the political sociology of the time. They sought to understand how interests and circumstances propelled people into activism, how available organizations shaped both new political selves as well as new strategic possibilities for collective action. As the sites for research multiplied, however, scholars questioned one of the central organizing assumptions of the first wave of social movement research, namely the distinction between social movements and "politics," the contrast of "contentious politics" and institutional politics. Increasingly, studies demonstrated that what had been taken as separate forms of political action, practiced by different sorts of people, were themselves elements of a common repertoire deployed in many societies. The classic cases for the analysis of revolution (e.g. 1789 in France) or the civil rights movement in the South or the student movement at a time when 21 was the voting age had started with Tilly's distinction between "incumbents" and "challengers." But new studies increasingly emphasized how different styles of politics were entwined in complex episodes of contention, both in legislatures and on the streets.

Mobilization into Participation

How can we explain why – and which – people participate in social activism? This is a central puzzle in the literature which has prompted much theoretical elaboration. But, as Ziad Munson (2008) contends in his study of pro-life activists, these arguments tend to be based on a core assumption: that ideas or interests precede (and explain) the decision to participate. One shortcoming of these arguments lies in the fact that many more people share the relevant attitudes than decide to participate – thus the standard model cannot explain which people participate among those who share particular ideas or attitudes. So what factors can explain why only a portion of those who support or oppose restrictions on gun purchases or protection of wetlands or provision of social services for the homeless choose to participate? To address this puzzle, scholars in both political science and political sociology have focused on network ties and invitations to participate as central to the explanation of who participates (Verba et al. 1995; see chapter 4). While such arguments provide somewhat more purchase on the question of which people become activists, the same problem recurs: many more people are connected by network ties or invited to join than actually participate.

In *The Making of Pro-Life Activists*, Ziad Munson challenges both the primacy of preferences and the adequacy of network ties in explaining who participates in social movements. Based on extensive observations and interviews of both pro-life activists and sympathetic non-participants in four cities, he documents how involvement in the movement flows from a combination of an invitation to participate with a turning point in an individual life. Contrary to the dominant model, pro-life beliefs often followed from participation as did transformation and deepening of religious beliefs. Even before the *Roe v. Wade* decision in 1974, one soon-to-be-activist attended legislative hearings on abortion due to the encouragement of her doctor: "she went out of a sense of personal obligation to ... a man who had helped her through a difficult pregnancy ... she agreed because she wanted to please someone she knew personally, not because she considered herself pro-life." At the legislative hearings, "she understood proponents of liberalizing abortion law to be arguing that abortion is needed to 'eliminate' disabled children and those conceived when a black man rapes a white woman" (2008: 18–19). Reversing the usual causal model that moves from preferences and interests to action, Munson found that "mobilization occurs when people are drawn into activism through organizational and relational ties, not when they form strong beliefs about abortion. Beliefs about abortion are often undeveloped, incoherent, and inconsistent until individuals become actively engaged with the movement" (2008: 20).

Munson's analysis contrasts with Nina Eliasoph's (1997) account of how citizens learned to focus only on those issues that were "close to home" and potentially influenced by civic action (see chapter 4 for the discussion of "rational apathy"). The pro-life movement, by comparison, effectively taught new participants to reshape their preferences by learning to care deeply about problems that might be distant from their everyday experience, echoing the practices of some of the earliest American social movements that generated a sense of personal moral responsibility to oppose slavery through powerful experiences of religious revival (Young 2006). Participation in the movement might then lead to further reconstructions of identity and transformation of network ties, notably as those led to activism were led in turn to renewed and deepened religious commitments (Munson 2008: 155–84).

Participation, of course, is not a one-time affair. Social movement scholars are interested not only in how and why non-participants become participants but when and where participants continue to participate. Here, just as in the literature on political socialization, organizational arrangements and culture turn out to be critical factors in whether an episode of participation translates into a career of activism. Dana Fisher explores this question in *Activism Inc.* (2006), focusing on a large, national organization that regularly recruits young people into summer positions soliciting funds in support of a variety of liberal causes. Informed by an archival reconstruction of the organization's history and strategy, Fisher gained access to a sample of one summer's cohort of participants, interviewing them early and late in the summer as well as following up with as many as could be located the following year. The results confound the stylized, optimistic reading of Tocqueville that has informed much of the work on social capital. Rather than participation breeding more participation, this experience of activism left many participants disillusioned and disconnected from political life, much as the participants in "empowerment projects" were civically energized only to feel disappointed and disrespected (Eliasoph 2011; chapter 4).

For Fisher, this finding prompted a comparative question. If this liberally oriented organization sustains a pattern of participation that is ultimately demobilizing, how can one explain the contrast with many conservative organizations which appear to translate youth activism into enduring commitment? The answer, she argues, lies in recognizing how different organizational models construct opportunities for careers in activism. Ironically, to the extent that her focal organization supported liberal causes but drew on a model of hierarchically coordinated door-to-door salesmanship, it provided few paths into more challenging forms of participation and few opportunities for each summer's cohort to engage meaningfully with the substance of causes for which they raised funds. A number of conservative organizations, by comparison, set up paths that led from the recruitment of college students to more challenging positions in policy institutes or party organizations. Such organizational choices shape the probabilities that political participation will result in people internalizing the sense that "being political" is an important source of identity.

The move from episodes of participation to careers of activism thus depends on a combination of transformations in identities and values along with organizational contexts that facilitate the movement from one protest to another, one cause to another, and one protest into a way of life. These effects are particularly striking in Doug McAdam's study of those who applied to participate in a civil rights project to register voters and staff "freedom schools" in Mississippi in the summer of 1964.

The Freedom Summer project for civil rights in Mississippi provides a powerful example of how the experience of participation can change the trajectory of individual lives. As McAdam explains, social science provides at least two different models for how this can happen. The first is conversion, "a radical transformation of a person's life, including their self-conception, networks of associations and larger world view." The second is an alternation between identities that are continuous with existing patterns of behavior and social roles. "The crucial difference," McAdam argues, "centers on the degree to which the change is continuous with the individual's previous life and conception of self" (1989: 745).

To assess whether movement participation can produce lasting change through a direct influence on the lives of participants, McAdam located and interviewed applicants to the

Freedom Summer project, both those who actually went to Mississippi and those who were accepted but were no-shows. It turned out that participants were much more active politically in the six years after the summer project, engaging in other civil rights efforts as well as the student, anti-war and women's liberation movements. A significant number found paid work "in the movement" and considered political "fit" in their choices of romantic partners (1989: 750). For McAdam, this represents a pattern of "alternation" in that participation in Freedom Summer did not leave the volunteers with a fully transformed pattern of life but did systematically shift the ways in which they made their ways through decisions about careers, marriage, and ongoing political engagement. The former volunteers were less likely to be married a number of years later and made lower incomes, but were more politically engaged. The veterans of Freedom Summer "left Mississippi not only more attitudinally disposed toward activism, but embedded in a set of relationships and an emerging activist subculture ideally suited to reinforce the process of personal change begun in Mississippi" (1989: 752). This experience of activism reverberated across the lives of the Freedom Summer volunteers.

Sometimes, however, individuals have little choice when it comes to activism. As research on the revolutions in France from 1789 through the nineteenth century has shown (chapter 3), the probabilities of mobilization and the ways in which interests were understood are powerfully shaped by the specific contexts in which actors find themselves as difficult times developed into crisis. In her compelling analysis of how women did or did not become active participants (either as guerrillas or collaborators) in the civil war that extended from 1979 to 1992 in El Salvador, Jocelyn Viterna (2013) asked how context influenced the paths taken by individuals. The often desperate choices imposed by a spreading conflict might be faced by women in villages not yet touched by war, in refugee camps, "repopulations," or even in guerrilla camps in the mountains. This analysis leads Viterna to an argument that differs in important ways from the arguments of political opportunity scholars with their assumption of a more-or-less rational and strategic actor just waiting for the moment: "Movements do not necessarily take off because a political opportunity makes success seem more plausible to potential participants. Rather, movements take off when *Changing macro-level environments reshape (1) the meanings of the identities that individuals hold, and (2) the memberships of the networks in which individuals are embedded*" (2013: 42; original emphasis). These reshapings were dramatic in many cases, with women finding their ways to service in guerrilla camps in the mountains, sometimes handling radios and serving in medical tents, sometimes bearing arms.

Yet Viterna's account of women in El Salvador's civil war leaves us with a paradox. For all the "gender-bending" qualities of women's participation during the civil war, the conclusion of the conflict (however troubled and uncertain) was followed by a re-imposition and intensification of the traditional gender order. Unlike the Freedom Summer volunteers who migrated to locales where political and social networks preserved and reinforced the impact of their participation and their orientation to activism, Viterna's former guerrillas often returned to civilian life along paths that broke their connections to their wartime comrades. This paradox raises a larger debate over the relation of disruption to political and social change.

On the one side is a common sense view that the scale of change is proportional to the scale of disruption. It is precisely this assumption that makes the outcome in El Salvador so surprising. If women were picking up guns and fighting on the front lines, surely that major deviation from expected gender roles would lead to some lasting transformation of the possibilities for female former guerrillas and for the women of El Salvador more generally? A second approach to the question of change makes exactly the opposite assumption. With its mascot as a mythical butterfly in China that flaps its wings setting off an escalating chain of events, this argument claims that small changes in initial conditions can produce large changes in outcomes.

Sociological arguments about change are best developed between these two extremes. Begin by asking about the character of order prior to some disruption (which itself may be understood as "external" or "internal"). What is the character of the disruption and how does it affect specific elements of the prior social order? What paths can be found from intense experiences of participation into more everyday politics in communities or routine elections? These questions point toward research on the organizational models and networks that are mobilized by social movements, the interactions of movements with "institutional politics," and the emergence of distinctive trajectories of change within different systems of political order (Clemens and Cook 1999).

Repertoires of Organization

Social movement scholarship often begins with a striking episode of change and then traces backward through history. While this might be critiqued as "selecting on the dependent variable," it can also be understood as a technique for understanding relatively rare but significant happenings. Medical doctors might begin with those afflicted by a complicated and dangerous epidemic in an effort to identify the source of the contagion and the mechanics of a mysterious disease, but this is understood as prelude to asking questions about who is exposed and, of those, who becomes infected. Such research designs are comparatively rare in social movement research (but see McAdam and Boudet 2012) and often remain focused on the question of mobilization and protest rather than outcomes of significant social change.

Take one particularly striking example of social change: a shift in the terms of the central social institution of marriage. Although there is ample historical reason to differ with the claim that marriage has always been between "one man and one woman" – there are too many examples of polygamous societies to sustain such an argument – it is nevertheless striking that marriage equality has been recognized for same-sex couples, when even a hint that one wanted – much less was part of – a same-sex relationship would have been cause for losing a job, social ostracism, and designation as a national security threat only decades earlier. How did those who were disadvantaged, excluded, and unrecognized mobilize to secure institutional recognition in this dramatic way?

An answer to this question begins with attention to the repertoires of contention or organization, the set of culturally familiar models that can be invoked to organize collective action and to signal how that action should be interpreted by others (Clemens 1997; Tilly 1995). Tracing the genealogy of gay and lesbian organizing in San Francisco, Elizabeth Armstrong (2002) highlights how different organizational models produced different patterns of political action and alliance across the decades after the Second World War. The earliest formal organizations named themselves in ways that protected the identity of groups that were outside the political system and keenly aware of the danger of prosecution in an era when homosexuality could be a basis for losing a job and social exclusion. The San Francisco chapter of the Mattachine Society (adopting the name of medieval masked groups that mocked the monarchs) was established by male homosexuals in 1953; lesbians founded the Daughters of Bilitis (echoing the language of the innumerable fraternal lodges established across the country) a few years later. These early organizations grew out of semi-private sites for sociability (an important source of social closure, see chapter 1), including bars and motorcycle clubs, and at times adopted the organizational structure of Communist Party cells in order to maximize security.

In time, inspired by the successes of the African American civil rights movement, these activists reconstituted themselves as "homophile," invoking a centralized interest-group model making claims for rights and intervening in the regulatory efforts of city and state government (Armstrong 2002: 41). But this approach foundered on a basic problem of sequence. How was it possible to make a claim to represent a group before the group "exists" in the sense of individuals recognizing themselves and others as members of the same category? Just as in the formation of national identity (see chapter 3), the construction of a collective identity was central to the process of reconfiguring political and social order.

As is often the case, the key to mobilizing was designation as a threat and the experience of repression. Those bars, which provided somewhat private sites for sociability, were also subject to regulation by the city's Alcoholic Beverage Control Department which ordered a series of raids; the city's police raided a New Year's Ball jointly sponsored by homophile organizations and leading civil rights figures from the city's establishment. The result was predictable: "thus were the pleasure seekers politicized" (Armstrong 2002: 49–51). These raids served as "signaling events" and, as in East Germany in 1989 (see chapter 3), they shifted the balance among exit, voice, and loyalty in people's political calculations. But to realize that shift, gay activists in San Francisco drew on an adjacent, and increasingly vibrant, movement taking root in the Bay Area: the New Left. Although its roots were in the student movement and the emerging counter-culture, the New Left provided cultural materials for reframing sexual identity as an interest and identity: "Based on the assumption that alienation is the fundamental problem with society and achieving authenticity the ultimate goal of progressive social change, the logic of identity politics transformed the meaning of secrecy about sexual identity. Homophile activists viewed privacy as necessary and self-protective.... The identity political logic provided the framework that defined public revelation of sexuality as both an important political act and a crucial step to psychological health" (2002: 57). New tactics centered on "coming out" in public and, in the process, made latent groups based on sexual identity increasingly visible to themselves, thereby changing the basis for subsequent "gay rights" organizing that lasted long after the decline of the New Left.

To explain the eventual success of these movements in transforming the categories and regulation of sexual identity, Armstrong draws on arguments about the transposition of models as a key form of political change (Sewell 1992; see chapter 4):

> Most of the time society is constituted by an interlocking network of fields, each organized by taken-for-granted rules. The institutionalized character of individual arenas and the collective weight of related fields reinforcing one another limit both what it is possible to think and what it is possible to do. Actors usually have a good idea of what kind of action is possible and what kind of action is not possible. These perceived limits shape what people can even imagine wanting. The more stable the interlocking set of fields, the more limited is cultural creativity. (Armstrong 2002: 58)

With this case for the conditions of cultural creativity, Armstrong provides an important alternative to Michael Mann's imagery of social power as organized through interlocking networks (1986; see chapter 1). While the linkage of networks may be a technique for combining and aggregating power, those combinations also represent points where distinctive fields come into contact, each potentially supporting a repertoire of action and organizing that might be transposed to destabilize some other field or to strengthen a mobilization by finding affinities across social movements (Jung et al. 2014). Among such points of contact, some of the most significant are those between social movement activity and institutional politics. Returning to those two models of change, sometimes social movements and revolutionary mobilization may take the form of catastrophic ruptures in existing systems of political and social ordering. But often mobilization moves within and along existing networks of political organization, unraveling, recombining, and displacing elements of earlier orders (Morris 1993) without producing a transformative change in the system as a whole.

Interactions between Contentious and Institutional Politics

As projects of mobilization, social movements can contribute to the work of building majorities and articulating interests and identities. In these ways, social movements are not only disruptive or contentious; they may also have an outsized impact on party strategy insofar as they represent "pre-constituted" blocs of voters and networks through which to mobilize participation and disseminate ways of framing public problems and policy solutions. In this fashion, the influence of social movements can be diffused and, possibly, even magnified through routine electoral politics inasmuch as political parties "articulate" citizens' understandings of their social identities, interests, and demands for different possible futures (de Leon et al. 2015; chapter 5). But the encounter with political parties may also transform – and perhaps demobilize – social movements as the work of alliance-building repositions movements as citizens consider the options of exit, voice, and loyalty.

One particularly dramatic example of such transformative interaction between contentious and institutional politics comes from a decidedly troubling corner of American political history: the political power of the Ku Klux Klan in the 1920s. Although it is difficult to grasp given the right–left spectrum and concerns for racial justice that inform so much of our thinking about contemporary politics, many Klansmen were also "progressive" in the specific sense that they were hostile toward big business and Wall Street. This hostility also encompassed the "high tariffs" that benefited manufacturers but fell hard upon farmers who exported crops and then purchased manufactured goods at prices that were kept high by tariff protections. People might be drawn to membership in the Klan for economic reasons as well as attraction to its organized racism and religious bigotry toward Catholics or, indeed, through network ties, invitations, and the appeal of social events. These intersecting lines of interest and grievance set up a distinctive context for political mobilization, particularly in Indiana which was home to the largest number of members of the Ku Klux Klan in the North in the decade after the First World War (Blee 1991). In what seems like a tale of strange bedfellows, many members of the Indiana Klan were initially favorable to the 1924 presidential campaign of Senator Robert La Follette of Wisconsin, still remembered as an icon of liberal progressivism. Yet, by the time of the election, the Klan supported Calvin Coolidge, candidate of the unquestionably pro-big business Republican Party (McVeigh et al. 2004: 654). What can explain this about-face? How does this add to our understanding of the relationship of preferences and participation already complicated by Ziad Munson's (2008) analysis of the pro-life movement?

To make sense of an outcome that is seemingly at odds with the original preferences of participants, McVeigh et al. focus our attention on the mobilizing or framing process, specifically on how processes similar to "social closure" (chapter 1) are set in motion by leaders to create new patterns of social solidarity: "One way of constructing and reinforcing collective identity boundaries is to emphasize the characteristics, traditions, and cultural values that distinguish supporters from others" (McVeigh et al. 2004: 656). But success in such efforts may have the effect of creating new lines of conflict with those who fall outside the mobilizing effort of the organizers. This sets up a challenge for movement activists: "They can attempt to expand broad support by being less exclusionary and adversarial, but they do so at the risk of losing their core constituency" (2004: 657). In a federal system, the potential benefits of alliance with the Klan in a state such as Indiana were outweighed by the consequences of how such an alliance was perceived outside the state, not only by those repulsed by the Klan's racism but by the large voting blocs that keyed on the Klan's hostility towards Catholics specifically and immigrants more generally: "The movement's exclusionary boundary construction meant that in many locations (particularly outside of Indiana) there would be significant political opposition to anyone aligned with the Klan" (2004: 678). To avoid such a taint, La Follette as well as the Democratic candidate explicitly disavowed the Klan, leaving it with no place to direct its electoral influence other than the pro-business Republican candidate who had remained silent: "By refusing to condemn the Klan, [Calvin] Coolidge risked losing votes among Catholics, immigrants, and African Americans but he also stood to benefit by picking up votes from the millions of Klan members throughout the nation. He also picked up votes from native-born white Protestants who were not members of the Klan, but were 'included' within the movement's boundary construction" (2004: 678).

The electoral dynamics around the Klan in 1924 illustrate how processes of social closure and boundary construction can set off shifting alliances that follow the logic of "the enemy of my enemy is my friend." Movements can also have consequences for party politics through a signaling function (chapter 3; Pfaff and Kim 2003), making visible new constituencies that might be courted either by profit-making firms or political entrepreneurs. Cristina Mora (2014) traces how ethnic activists constructed the identity category of "Hispanic" by working across fields, pushing the US Census to change how it counted members by ethnic or racial identity, which in turn made it possible to argue that broadcasters and retailers had a category to target in their coverage and advertisements, and, in time, as a highly relevant constituency for local, state, and national politics.

There are risks as well as opportunities when movements orient themselves to electoral politics, either as constituencies to be courted or as active participants in nominating processes and elections. Engagement, however arm's length, between movements and parties can also reshape the ways in which participants imagine the connections between their activism and political outcomes or broader social change. In a study of the anti-war movement against the US invasions of Iraq and Afghanistan in the wake of the 9/11 terrorist attacks, Michael Heaney and Fabio Rojas (2015) document movement–party dynamics that resembled those observed in the Indiana Klan of 1924, although the issues at stake and the political commitments of the actors were very different: "political parties with social movement constituencies usually broaden their platforms to appeal to a wider spectrum of voters. This broadening pulls the party's agenda away from the social movement's goals, which often lie at the radical edges of politics. Thus, the partisan approach creates pressures to moderate issue positions, whereas the issue purity of the movement approach tends to fall short of majority support" (2015: 20; on party dynamics, see Downs 1957). In one reading, this might be taken as a guarantee of failure and disappointment on both sides of the relationship between movement actors and party activists. But, as Heaney and Rojas argue, the interaction itself may transform one or both of those involved. Ultimately, the anti-war movement supported the nomination of Barack Obama as the Democrat's presidential candidate in 2008. But, having put "their guy" in office, movement activists then demobilized either out of the expectation that the powers of the presidency would be sufficient to end the war or a desire to avoid discrediting their candidate. Ironically, mobilization that was "successful" in terms of influencing the nominating process proved incapable of securing the military withdrawal it sought, although Obama's foreign policy stance led to significant if not total reductions of force and an aversion to additional military engagements, at least by conventional forces. Yet, as Obama neared the end of his second term, the questions of whether to send additional military forces to intervene in Middle Eastern conflicts were still very much on the agenda, bringing into question the capacity of impressive protest movements to secure substantial and lasting change.

The de-energizing effects of expanded political access are not unique to the anti-war movement that emerged with the prospect of a US invasion of Iraq and Afghanistan. A decade earlier, the election of a new Democratic president had a similar impact on the mobilization against AIDS. As Deborah Gould argues in *Moving Politics* (2009), the intense direct action campaigns waged by ACT-UP chapters across the nation were already buffeted by disappointing reports from medical researchers that the hoped-for treatments and possibly even cures would not materialize in the near future. After years of activism fueled by the hope of saving the lives of friends, lovers and families, an emerging sense of despair made the possibility of turning to a friendlier national government appear as a much more appealing option. And, to the extent that the Clinton administration did indeed present new opportunities for engagement through institutional politics and policy development, these opportunities were coupled to expectations for a more moderated, "professional" etiquette for working with experts in public health and biomedical research. The profound emotional dynamics of grief, love, anger, hope, and despair fed shifts in the form and focus of activism as well as the response from policy-makers and political officials.

Social Movements and Trajectories of Change

Tracing the connections between social movements and social change requires going beyond simple models of cause and effect: the more protests, the more change. With an eye to the importance of identities, interests, networks, resources, and relations to institutional politics, it is clear that social movement participation may contribute to social change along multiple paths. Participation can have direct effects on individuals, changing their attitudes, behaviors, and values as has been documented by scholars such as Doug McAdam, Ziad

Munson, and Jocelyn Viterna. Here, the key effects are not understood in terms of whether or not a movement's goals were attained. The impact is on the participants themselves.

A second path to lasting social change works through broader shifts in attitudes rather than via the impact on the individual lives of participants. In a striking piece of counterfactual analysis, Clem Brooks (2000) makes a case for the importance of the movements of the 1960s on those who did not participate. Arguing against the claim that the substantial changes observed in attitudes toward civil rights (for African Americans, women, gays and lesbians) represents only a "superficial liberalism," Brooks proceeds by a statistical version of counterfactual reasoning to demonstrate that these lasting distributions of attitudes are associated with important changes in how citizens make choices among political parties in presidential elections. Because those with liberal attitudes toward civil rights are more likely to vote for the Democratic presidential candidate, to the extent that movement activities shifted the distribution of attitudes in the electorate, those movements contributed to political change through the voting booth. Brooks concludes that "Without [liberal] changes in civil rights attitudes, Democratic candidates would have lost *every* presidential election between 1972 and 1996" (2000: 500). Here, movements shift attitudes not only for participants but also within the broader electorate, altering the terrain upon which parties compete for office.

Finally, social movements and insurgencies may have lasting consequences through the creation of new social contexts. As Elizabeth Armstrong demonstrated in her study of gay and lesbian organizing in San Francisco, movements did not only secure recognition or policy change, they also fueled the creation of new kinds of organizations and communities. In time, these then served as contexts for still more novel forms of mobilization as part of an extended sequence of movement events that eventually fed into institutional politics, through initiatives and election of candidates and through the courts, producing the recognition of new rights in the established institution of marriage.

As should be clear, research on social movements speaks to the most central questions for political sociology. What is the balance between factors that create pressures for the restoration or reproduction of an existing organization of power versus those that propagate and amplify change? How can we understand why sometimes people simply live with anger and the experience of oppression, sometimes they mobilize without producing change, and sometimes, although less frequently than activists would hope, mobilization leads to significant transformations of political institutions and the invention of new ways of ordering political power?

7
Transnationalism and the Future(s) of Political Order

Although the early history of political order produced an explosion of inventive forms, over the past few centuries the dynamics of empires and nation-states – as well as nation-states within empires – have defined the dominant outlines of global political organization. But if the decades after the Second World War represented a sort of high water mark for the nation-state, the currents of change have shifted again, challenging the boundaries of the nation-state and generating new forms of political order. As John Markoff (2013: 13) explains, in contemporary political discussions, "the nation of delimited territoriality has remained a central assumption. In the early twenty-first century, however, there are many reasons to anticipate a major conceptual shift. The web of transnational connection, the development of transnational structures of decision making (from the European Union to the International Monetary Fund), and the vast disparity of wealth and power among nation-states are calling into questions the democracy in them."

One source of change is obvious. In an increasingly globalized world – measured in terms of travel, communication, culture, or trade – crises, grievances, and aspirations are not easily contained within nation-states. In Michael Mann's terminology, key social cages are becoming less self-contained. Protests mobilize against multinational corporations and free trade pacts, for or against immigrants seeking work and those seeking political refuge. Whether one is looking down the "fence" at the US–Mexico border, at a plunging stock market destabilized by far-away events, at reports of an epidemic spread by way of international flights, or a plume of polluted air or radioactive pollution driven by the winds, it is clear that economic, political, and environmental processes cross-cut national boundaries.

Although these phenomena are not new, they appear faster, stronger and clearer in an age of new communication technologies, more rapid news cycles, and accelerated transportation. All of these developments require us to revisit the question of the dominance of the nation-state as the model for political order and to ask a new set of questions about the possibilities for political mobilization and action. How can political action be organized across national borders? How can actors within national politics address problems that cross national borders? And, what kind of politics is possible in opposition to international systems of private and public actors subject to a complex mix of regulation and market dynamics?

World Society and State-Building

The process of state-building has not been contained by the boundaries around states. To revisit the argument of Charles Tilly (chapter 2), competition within systems of states drives individual projects of state-building within territorial boundaries. In order to meet or even overcome the threat of an adjacent political order, any actor who seeks to build a state must advance their own efforts to centralize control and mobilize resources. As states develop in competition with one another, however, there is a question of why they so often come to resemble one another. More specifically, why is it that the nation-state became the dominant model for political organization, replicated around the world, recognized by other states, and required as a condition for representation in a growing number of international governing organizations such as – note the name – the United Nations.

John Meyer and his colleagues have developed a powerful theoretical model, supported by an ongoing, collaborative construction of a cross-national, longitudinal data set that tracks state policies, political institutions, economic and demographic factors, adoption of treaties, membership in international organizations, and much more. Their core argument takes the following form:

> Many features of the contemporary nation-state derive from worldwide models constructed and propagated through global cultural and associational processes. These models and the purposes they reflect (e.g. equality, socioeconomic progress, human development) are highly rationalized, articulated, and often surprisingly consensual. Worldwide models define and legitimate agendas for local action, shaping the structures and policies of nation-states and other national and local actors in virtually all of the domains of rationalized social life – business, politics, education, medicine, science, and even the family and religion. (Meyer et al. 1997: 144–5)

In this argument, the core claim is made for a "higher order" or top-down effect, a central feature of sociological institutionalism (see chapter 5). In a strong version of a cultural argument, Meyer and his collaborators argue that there is a shared set of beliefs or expectations about what a state should look like (including the expectation that it will be a state coupled to some sense of categorical membership, a "nation-state") and what elements it will include. No matter what the demographic, environmental, or economic situation, a newly established state is expected to have some designated head of government, distinctive currency and stamps, a set of ministries, a designated central place (often marked by a particularly impressive airport with a set of highways fanning out from it toward something, whether a major city or a graveled road heading out toward the horizon). Consequently, the key empirical support for this argument takes the form of findings of "no association" between functional requirements and formal political organization. In other words, the likelihood that a nation will have a system of graded education that is required for children from approximately 5 to 16 years of age is not statistically associated with its level of economic development or even of literacy (Meyer et al. 1992). Nation-states adopt these policies because they are part of what is expected of a nation-state.

This strong argument for conceptualizing nation-states as models embedded in a world culture contrasts sharply with ways of thinking about the process of state-building and national-imaging that we have encountered in earlier chapters: Tilly's focus on the instrumental efforts of political actors to centralize power, mobilize resources, and make war; Elazar's imagery of political organization as springing from durable cultural and religious traditions of particular peoples; or the multiple literatures – including analyses of empires, trading networks, and dependent development – that trace national development at nodes within global flows of trade and competition.

The shift from nation-states to global processes, however, does not always take such an insistently cultural form. Whereas Meyer and his collaborators envisioned world society or world culture as a system of shared meanings and expectations, others have theorized a "world polity" in which efforts at mobilization and the exercise of voice are not constrained by national borders. Neither, of course, are the problems and opportunities that provoke political action.

Democratic Responses to Transnational Issues

A striking example of the unexpected political dynamics that play out across national borders is provided by Rhonda Evans and Tamara Kay (2008) in their comparative study of labor and environmental activism during the negotiation and adoption of the North American Free Trade Agreement (NAFTA). Intended to create a three-nation free trade zone – encompassing Mexico, the United States, and Canada – the politics of NAFTA represented a threat to victories that activists had already secured within their own national polities. Union leaders were worried that wage agreements and workplace regulation would be undermined by competition from Mexican workers; environmental activists sought to protect regulatory regimes embedded in national, state, and local laws.

If we think back to the basic models in which the distribution of electoral support determines policy outcomes (see chapter 4), a fairly simple prediction follows. We should expect the more powerful set of activists – measured in terms of some combination of membership, financial resources, and political networks – to be most successful in minimizing the damage imposed by a free trade agreement. In the terms of "resource mobilization" theory (see chapter 6), organized labor would be considered unquestionably more powerful than the network of environmental activists and nonprofit organizations. Yet, surprisingly, environmentalists came out with the better results in terms of the strength of the "side agreements" that were included in the NAFTA treaty. That "strength" is embodied in the recognition of their claims as legitimate as well as in activists' access to negotiators. The result was the creation of "new transnational adjudicatory institutions and mechanisms of enforcement" (Evans and Kay 2008: 970–1). Environmental activists were able to reframe "the environment" as a trade issue and thereby to subject trade negotiators to new sources of political pressure. Rather than trying to kill the treaty altogether, which was the strategy of many leading labor organizations, environmental activists mobilized from the start to influence the content of side agreements to a treaty that they assumed would be adopted.

A second example of how social movements have been able to shape, if far from entirely determine, the shape of transnational agreements comes from the emergence of new systems of *private* regulation of labor and environmental conditions in the forestry and clothing industries. As Tim Bartley demonstrates (2007), the issues at stake closely resembled those central to the NAFTA negotiations. There was also a similar pattern of results: somewhat stronger outcomes for sustainable forestry where environmental claims were important; somewhat weaker for apparel manufacturing where arguments about labor rights and regulations were central. But, in contrast to the mobilization around NAFTA, activism followed very different political pathways and involved different sets of actors. On the social movement side, the forestry mobilization involved environmentalists but also woodworkers and conservationists. The "anti-sweatshop" movement included not only labor rights activists but also consumer activists. In an even more striking contrast to

NAFTA, elected officials were less of a presence; national governments were constrained by their prior adoption of free trade agreements that limited their ability to sanction other governments for their economic practices. Finally, private corporations were prominent players in these conflicts, both as targets and as sometimes reluctant allies.

For Bartley, the puzzle was to understand what generated a new system of private economic regulation represented by "seals of approval" (for sustainable forestry, for non-sweatshop clothing, for "dolphin-safe" tuna) along with regimes of inspection and certification. Issues that first appeared in the context of trade agreements between nations migrated to consumer and environmental domains in a process of "forum shifting." Firms that were downstream in a system of production – clothing retailers, home construction chains – could be persuaded to put pressure in turn on the producers of running shoes or managers of commercial forests. Bartley argues that these new regulatory systems cannot be explained purely as efforts by firms to solve market-based problems but that they "reflect the negotiated settlements and institution-building projects that arise out of conflicts involving states, NGOs (nongovernmental organizations), and other nonmarket actors, as well as firms" (Bartley 2007: 299). In effect, this system of private regulation is an example of the politics of the second-best: "the institutional entrepreneurship of these NGOs grew out of failures in intergovernmental arenas and a strategy of forum shifting" (2007: 332).

Bartley, as well as Evans and Kay, describes a process of change already familiar from earlier discussions of social movements (chapter 6). If, following Elizabeth Armstrong, we envision society as "constituted by an interlocking network of fields, each organized by taken-for-granted rules" (2002: 58), the overlaps, boundaries, and intersections of those fields provide opportunities for mobilized activists to try to change the terms of regulation and participation in policy-making. As Bartley concludes, "the existence of a complex, multilevel institutional environment, with *multiple* arenas, allows this type of institutionally embedded agency to generate some degree of *change* rather than just reproduction of the existing social order" (2007: 311).

Mobilization across Borders

With the appearance of new forms of regulation and coordination, it is tempting to think of transnational politics as something new or, at least, something distinctive to the decades after the Second World War that saw the establishment of organizations such as the United Nations and its surrounding array of agencies and commissions. But, as Margaret Keck and Kathryn Sikkink (1998: 39) document, modern networks of transnational advocacy can be traced to much earlier mobilizations to end slavery and the slave trade, to outlaw footbinding of women as well as female circumcision. These mobilizations followed, in many cases, the networks of colonization, trade, and cultural exchange that were constituted by empires as systems of political and economic order.

Peter Stamatov (2010) reinforces this critique of the literature on transnational advocacy as much too presentist in its focus on the twentieth century. Taking Charles Tilly as his primary foil, he argues that historical research on the origins of social movements is too instinctively secular and thereby ignores the central role of religion as a matrix for new forms of political organizing (but see Young 2006). These two limitations of existing arguments trace to the same argument which located the origins of the modern social movement as a response to the emergence of the national state (Tilly 1995). Instead of focusing within national borders, however, Stamatov makes a case for empire as the matrix within which new forms of mobilization emerged: "Following distinctively religious interests in their confrontations with other imperial actors, these radicalized religious actors mobilized to defend the welfare of actual and potential converts to Christianity among geographically and culturally distant populations that had been drawn into the orbit of European imperialism" (2010: 608). Thus the structure of empire as a system of political order did not dictate that the only response would be the kind of dehumanization of the colonized that provoked Fanon's critique (chapter 2). Different actors, with distinctive cultural commitments grounded in religion, developed as a counterforce to the extractive projects of imperial economies.

Having advanced these two critiques, Stamatov has set the stage for an engagement with some of the figures who currently dominate historical sociology. Evoking Michael Mann's imagery of the intersection of diverse networks distinguished by a particular resource base, Stamatov's research suggests how much leverage we can gain by noticing that such intersections may not be fully accomplished but instead constitute durable zones of contention within which new political forms may develop: "Driven by specifically religious interests – the spread of Christianity and the salvation of souls – religious actors did not initially pursue political activities. They embarked on a course of political advocacy only after encountering irreconcilable conflicts with opposing secular networks that they perceived as undermining their evangelization and violating Christian ethics" (2010: 615). As studies of transnational advocacy have demonstrated, the structures of empire and systems of states in conflict and competition regularly produce such mobilizations. As importantly, sometimes those mobilizations against existing transnational arrangements of power produce the seeds of new forms of political order.

From World Society to World Polity

Many have been tempted to invoke a global system of politics simply by endorsing some concept of "world citizenry" in which something like the United Nations functions as a higher-order equivalent of a national legislature. It is not enough, however, to declare a "world polity" and then to assume that this guarantees a functional equivalent of a more-or-less democratic system of representation and responsive government. Even if analogues to certain elements of national polities can be found at the global level, others are strikingly absent. Missing are at least two pieces: "a mechanism by which the world polity can reach its citizens (rather than touching their lives only indirectly, by enforcing their rights as citizens of nation-states); and ... some mode of democratic participation by the individuals and groups who make up the citizens of this transnational political order" (Watkins et al. 2012: 306).

One possible infrastructure for such a transnational political order can be found in the burgeoning population of not-for-profit (the US term of choice) or non-governmental (the term used in much of the rest of the world) organizations. Some of these organizations are involved in the kinds of transnational advocacy discussed above; others define their mission in terms of humanitarian relief, development aid, medical missions, and charity of all sorts.

The challenges posed to the nonprofit world as a kind of polity are highlighted through a comparison with the problems of empire discussed in chapter 2. Just as the "company men" sent to the Dutch East Indies were agents of "principals" back home in the Netherlands (Adams 1996), these nonprofit organizations can be understood as agents of donors, whether private individuals, foundations, or governments. But, in an age infused with democratic norms, these nonprofits are in some sense also responsible to the communities and populations that they intend to serve. Thus "a key problem for foreign donors is that they cannot actually reach their intended beneficiaries directly, but rather have to act through an 'aid chain' of other organizations" (Watkins et al. 2012: 287). This dependence is often managed through a bureaucracy of accounting or "metrics"; this in turn creates incentives for intermediary NGOs to focus their attention on projects that will produce the kind of results appreciated by donors rather than being guided by some other standard, whether of support within the beneficiary population or some assessment of absolute need (Krause 2014). In this way, calls for "accountability" and "measurable results" produce a distinctive form of policy feedback (see chapter 5; Watkins et al. 2012: 299) in which effort is directed to problems that are difficult but "solvable" in terms of some system of documentation.

Because intermediaries cannot count on continued support from donors, they are attuned to the expectations of those donors as much as to the participation and preferences of the intended beneficiaries. So for all that NGOs are often linked to discourses of civic engagement, they do not necessarily function as elements in some chain of political participation. As Watkins and her colleagues explain (2012: 296): "The basic dilemma of NGO goals arises from the paradoxical nature of altruism itself: The altruist, acting for the benefit of another, may or may not be providing something others really want ... If the recipient of altruism cannot get what she needs on her own, then it is not her definition of her needs, but those of the altruist, that prevail." Awareness of the workings of power within the system of NGOs leaves us with the question of the extent to which meaningfully democratic or participatory politics is possible in a system of "organized altruism" that extends across borders.

A second, and perhaps more obvious, way of moving toward a "world polity" is to construct ever more encompassing international organizations, whether the United Nations with its near (but not quite) universality or specifically regional entities such as the trade-focused NAFTA or the much more ambitious project of building and expanding the European Union. These projects produce, in turn, new patterns of politics with citizens of many European nations mobilizing to protest at EU headquarters in Brussels in an effort to counter what many perceive to be a "democratic deficit," although much political activity remains national in focus (Fligstein 2008: 207–41). Corporations, however, have reorganized themselves along European lines (Fligstein 2008: 88–122) such that their activities more easily escape nationally specific systems of regulation. Through EU-level agencies, firms may push for policies that undercut the redistributive projects central to European welfare states (chapter 5), generating new sources of grievance and unraveling the solidarities that universal systems of social provision had sustained (Berezin 2009). Such mismatches produce more critique and repeated prompts to come up with novel governing arrangements. In these efforts, many of the processes familiar from studies of nation-building and nationalism (chapter 2) reappear.

A third path is defined by the dynamic intersection of transnational or global norms and law-making within nation-states. In the same way that movement activists and corporate actors shaped new systems of private regulation (Bartley 2007), corporate actors and political elites operate across national and global arenas to craft and promote a convergence of regulatory concepts despite persisting differences in implementation (Halliday and Carruthers 2007). Yasemin Soysal (1994) documents a similar combination of convergence at the level of global norms and treaties with durable national-level differences in the translation of norms into practices and political settlements around the issue of citizenship rights for guest workers and immigrants. At each subsequent round in "recursive" processes of law-making, the gaps between global norms and national settlements then shape the opportunities for new activism.

Transnational Problems as Challenges to Democracy

The project of constructing a "world polity" or simply a more adequate method for coping with global challenges becomes even more challenging when there is no reason to assume altruism on the part of those who control key transnational relationships and flows. As John Markoff (2013: 24) argues, "the growing structure of transnational loci of decision making with little accountability to those affected by those decisions seems likely to call into question the adequacy of the core notion of a self-governing people on a delimited territory." In recent years, protestors around the world have encountered both the unresponsiveness of their own governments and the elusiveness of those controlling the making of key decisions, whether in the private executive suites of multinational corporations or the exclusive social gatherings of the global political-economic-entertainment elite.

Given the powerful cultural, economic, and technological forces driving this globalization, is this erosion of democratic politics inevitable? Or, as John Markoff argues, is it possible to imagine a transnational democratic order, to engage in the kind of cultural creativity with respect to the forms of poli-cal ordering that have characterized earlier mc cal history? Recalling how the founders of tl democratic republics – in the United States and selective use of ancient models of democracy, return to basic questions about the character anc of political order: Who is a member? With what rights? How would representatives or leaders be chosen? How would the tension between political equality and economic inequality be managed? Without answering these questions definitively, he makes a case for re-imagining democratic politics by pointing to a now-familiar feedback mechanism: the mobilization of social movements and the expression of discontent:

> Democracy seems inherently dynamic because it nurtures social movements energized by disappointment with the inadequately democratic character of actual institutions, including the boundaries of inclusion and exclusion; because its diverse claims are often contradictory, allowing very diverse movements to claim the democratic label; because powerholders find it helps them to claim that political arrangements that secure their power are "democratic," however inegalitarian and oppressive they may be; and because antidemocratic movements are nurtured along with movements for alternative democratic visions. (Markoff 2013: 19)

This leaves us with a final large question. Armed with tools from political sociology, what expectations can be generated about the kinds of politics that are produced by the mismatch between the scale of problems and the territory of democratic political orders? If, as so many scholars have argued, the character of political ordering is increasingly distant from the mechanisms of democratic responsibility associated with many nation-states, is it possible to imagine that some "common identity can emerge as the result of common subjection to the same political authority." Recalling Tilly's analysis of democratization, Markoff speculates that "the construction of an effective authoritarian transnational order may make the later development of a democratic one more possible, rather analogous to the national histories of Western Europe in which states generally got much stronger before they got more democratic" (2013: 29).

To the extent that globalization creates new patterns of circulation, it may have the same sort of impact that Benedict Anderson found in the curtailed "administrative pilgrimages" of *creoles* of pure Spanish descent born in imperial territories beyond the Iberian peninsula (chapter 2). The experience of sharing trajectories and becoming enmeshed in new networks may have a primarily deconstructive effect, loosening ties to national identity and nation-based solidarities. But, just perhaps, there may also be social materials here that can be used to develop new forms of social closure and solidarity that would sustain political mobilizations along non-national dimensions. As Markoff concludes, "recall that in imagining what a more democratic national state might be, the early modern democrats, faithful as they were to the Athenian model, on one important arena broke with it completely. They forced wholly new institutions of government.... Now we need to look beyond that national state with equal creativity" (Markoff 2013: 31). These possibilities and emerging trajectories of change cannot be understood solely by analyzing distributions of current preferences or the regularities of existing institutions. The core contribution of political sociology is to direct our attention to the opportunities for change that can be found in the situations we confront and to the materials – networks, organizing resources, local cultures, and possible alliances – out of which new political orders might be built.

References

Abrams, Philip. 1988 [1977]. "Notes on the Difficulty of Studying the State," *Journal of Historical Sociology* 1 (1): 58–89.

Adams, Julia. 1994. "The Familial State: Elite Family Practices and State-Making in the Early Modern Netherlands," *Theory and Society* 23 (4): 505–39.

Adams, Julia. 1996. "Principals and Agents, Colonialists and Company Men: The Decay of Colonial Control in the Dutch East Indies," *American Sociological Review* 61 (1): 12–28.

Alexander, Michelle. 2010. *The New Jim Crow: Mass Incarceration in the Age of Colorblindness*. New York: New Press.

Almond, Gabriel Abraham, and Sidney Verba. 1965. *The Civic Culture: Political Attitudes and Democracy in Five Nations, An Analytic Study*. Boston, MA: Little, Brown.

Anderson, Benedict. 1991 [1983]. *Imagined Communities: Reflections on the Origin and Spread of Nationalism*. London: Verso.

Armstrong, Elizabeth. 2002. *Forging Gay Identities: Organizing Sexuality in San Francisco, 1950–1994*. Chicago, IL: University of Chicago Press.

Ash, Timothy Garton. 1990. "The Revolution of the Magic Lantern," *The New York Review of Books*, January 18.

Bachrach, Peter, and Morton S. Baratz. 1962. "Two Faces of Power," *American Political Science Review* 56 (4): 947–52.

Baker, Jean H. 1983. *Affairs of Party: The Political Culture of Northern Democrats in the Mid-Nineteenth Century*. Ithaca, NY: Cornell University Press.

Barkey, Karen. 2008. *Empire of Difference: The Ottomans in Comparative Perspective*. New York: Cambridge University Press.

Bartley, Tim. 2007. "Institutional Emergence in an Era of Globalization: The Rise of Transnational Private Regulation of Labor and Environmental Conditions," *American Journal of Sociology* 113 (2): 297–351.

Bendix, Reinhard. 1964. *Nation-Building and Citizenship*. Berkeley, CA: University of California Press.

Berelson, Bernard, Paul Lazarsfeld, and William McPhee. 1954. *Voting*. Chicago, IL: University of Chicago Press.

Berezin, Mabel. 2009. *Illiberal Politics in Neoliberal Times: Culture, Security and Populism in the New Europe*. New York: Cambridge University Press.

Berry, Jeffrey M. and Sarah Sobieraj. 2011. "Understanding the Rise of Talk Radio," *PS: Political Science & Politics* 44 (4): 762–7.

Blee, Kathleen. 1991. *Women of the Ku Klux Klan: Racism and Gender in the 1920s*. Berkeley, CA: University of California Press.

Bourdieu, Pierre. 1994. "Rethinking the State: Genesis and Structure of the Bureaucratic Field," *Sociological Theory* 12 (1): 1–18.

Breen, T.H. 2004. *The Marketplace of Revolution: How Consumer Politics Shaped American Independence*. New York: Oxford University Press.

Brewer, John. 1988. *The Sinews of Power: War, Money and the English State, 1688–1783*. Cambridge, MA: Harvard University Press.

Brinton, Crane. 1965. *The Anatomy of Revolution*. New York: Vintage Books.

Brooks, Clem. 2000. "Civil Rights Liberalism and the Suppression of a Republican Political Realignment in the United States, 1972 to 1996," *American Sociological Review* 65 (4): 483–505.

Brubaker, Rogers. 1996. *Nationalism Reframed: Nationhood and the National Question in the New Europe*. Cambridge: Cambridge University Press.

Burns, Nancy, Kay Lehman Schlozman, and Sidney Verba. 2001. *The Private Roots of Public Action: Gender, Equality, and Political Participation*. Cambridge, MA: Harvard University Press.

Calhoun, Craig. 1983. "The Radicalism of Tradition: Community Strength or Venerable Disguise and Borrowed Language?" *American Journal of Sociology* 88 (5): 886–914.

Campbell, Andrea Louise. 2003. *How Policies Make Citizens: Senior Political Activism and the American Welfare State*. Princeton, NJ: Princeton University Press.

Campbell, Angus, Philip E. Converse, Warren E. Miller, and Donald E. Stokes. 1960. *The American Voter*. New York: Wiley.

Chibber, Vivek. 2003. *Locked in Place: State-Building and Late Industrialization in India*. Princeton, NJ: Princeton University Press.

Clemens, Elisabeth S. 1993. "Organizational Repertoires and Institutional Change: Women's Groups and the Transformation of American Politics, 1890–1920," *American Journal of Sociology* 98 (4): 755–98.

Clemens, Elisabeth S. 1996. "Organizational Form as Frame: Collective Identity and Political Strategy in the American Labor Movement," in D. McAdam, J. McCarthy, and M. Zald (eds) *Comparative Perspectives on Social Movements: Opportunities, Mobilizing Structures, and Cultural Framings*. New York: Cambridge University Press, pp. 205–26.

Clemens, Elisabeth S. 1997. *The People's Lobby: Organizational Innovation and the Rise of Interest Group Politics in the United States, 1890–1925*. Chicago, IL: University of Chicago Press.

Clemens, Elisabeth. 2005. "Logics of History? Agency, Multiplicity, and Incoherence in the Explanation of Change," in Julia Adams, Elisabeth S. Clemens, and Ann Shola Orloff (eds) *Remaking Modernity: Politics, History, and Sociology*. Durham, NC: Duke University Press.

Clemens, Elisabeth, and James Cook. 1999. "Politics and Institutionalism: Explaining Durability and Change," *Annual Review of Sociology* 25: 441–66.

Cohen, Cathy. 1999. *The Boundaries of Blackness: AIDS and the Breakdown of Black Politics*. Chicago, IL: University of Chicago Press.

Collins, Randall. 1980. "Weber's Last Theory of Capitalism: A Systematization," *American Sociological Review* 45: 925–42.

Crozier, Michel. 1964. *The Bureaucratic Phenomenon*. Chicago, IL: University of Chicago Press.

Darwin, John. 2009. *The Empire Project: The Rise and Fall of the British World-System, 1830–1970*. New York: Cambridge University Press.

de Leon, Cedric, Manali Desai, and Cihan Tuğal. 2015. *Building Blocs: How Parties Organize Society*. Stanford, CA: Stanford University Press.

DeSilver, Drew. 2015. "US voter turnout trails most developed countries," Pew Research Center, Fact-tank, May 6.

de Tocqueville, Alexis. 2004. *Democracy in America*, trans. Arthur Goldhammer. New York: Library of America.

Diamond, Jared. 1997. *Guns, Germs, and Steel: The Fates of Human Societies*. New York: W.W. Norton.

Domhoff, G. William. 1967. *Who Rules America?* Englewood Cliffs, NJ: Prentice-Hall.

Domhoff, G. William. 1996. *State Autonomy or Class Dominance?: Case Studies on Policy Making in America.* New York: Aldine de Gruyter.

Downing, Brian M. 1992. *The Military Revolution and Political Change: Origins of Democracy and Autocracy in Early Modern Europe.* Chicago, IL: University of Chicago Press.

Downs, Anthony. 1957. *An Economic Theory of Democracy.* New York: Harper and Row.

Durkheim, Emile. 1964. *The Division of Labor in Society.* Glencoe, IL: The Free Press.

Edelman, Lauren B., Christopher Uggen, and Howard S. Erlanger. 1999. "The Endogeneity of Legal Regulation: Grievance Procedures as Rational Myth," *American Journal of Sociology* 105 (2): 406–54.

Elazar, Daniel J. 1975. "The American Cultural Matrix," in Daniel J. Elazar and Joseph Zikmund II (eds) *The Ecology of American Political Culture.* New York: Thomas Y. Crowell, pp. 13–42.

Eliasoph, Nina. 1997. " 'Close to Home': The Work of Avoiding Politics," *Theory and Society* 26 (5): 605–47.

Eliasoph, Nina. 1998. *Avoiding Politics: How Americans Produce Apathy in Everyday Life.* New York: Cambridge University Press.

Eliasoph, Nina. 2011. *Making Volunteers: Civic Life After Welfare's End.* Princeton, NJ: Princeton University Press.

Ertman, Thomas. 1997. *Birth of the Leviathan: Building States and Regimes in Medieval and Early Modern Europe.* New York: Cambridge University Press.

Esping-Andersen, Gøsta. 1990. *The Three Worlds of Welfare Capitalism.* Princeton, NJ: Princeton University Press.

Evans, Peter. 1995. *Embedded Autonomy: States and Industrial Transformation.* Princeton, NJ: Princeton University Press.

Evans, Peter, and James E. Rauch. 1999. "Bureaucracy and Growth: A Cross-National Analysis of the Effects of 'Weberian' State Structures on Economic Growth," *American Sociological Review* 64 (5): 748–65.

Evans, Rhonda, and Tamara Kay. 2008. "How Environmentalists 'Greened' Trade Policy: Strategic Action and the Architecture of Field Overlap," *American Sociological Review* 73 (6): 970–91.

Fanon, Frantz. 2004 [1961]. *The Wretched of the Earth*, trans. Richard Philcox. New York: Grove Press.

Ferree, Myra Marx, William Anthony Gamson, Jürgen Gerhards, and Dieter Rucht. 2002. *Shaping Abortion Discourse: Democracy and the Public Sphere in Germany and the United States*. New York: Cambridge University Press.

Fiorina, Morris P., and Samuel J. Abrams. 2008. "Political Participation in the American Public," *Annual Review of Political Science* 11: 563–88.

Fisher, Dana R. 2006. *Activism Inc.: How the Outsourcing of Grassroots Campaigns Is Strangling Progressive Politics in America*. Palo Alto, CA: Stanford University Press.

Fligstein, Neil. 2008. *Euro-Clash: The EU, European Identity, and the Future of Europe*. New York: Oxford University Press.

Fortner, Michael J. 2015. *Black Silent Majority: The Rockefeller Drug Laws and the Politics of Punishment*. Cambridge, MA: Harvard University Press.

Foucault, Michel. 2010. *The Birth of Biopolitics: Lectures at the Collège de France, 1978–1979*. New York: Picador.

Fox, Cybelle. 2012. *Three Worlds of Relief: Race, Immigration, and the American Welfare State from the Progressive Era to the New Deal*. Princeton, NJ: Princeton University Press.

Frank, Thomas. 2004. *What's the Matter with Kansas? How Conservatives Won the Heart of America*. New York: Metropolitan Books.

Fraser, Nancy. 1990. "Struggle Over Needs: Outline of a Socialist-Feminist Critical Theory of Late-Capitalist Political Culture," in Linda Gordon (ed.) *Women, the State, and Welfare*. Madison, WI: University of Wisconsin Press.

Freeman, Jo. 1974. "The Tyranny of Structurelessness," *The Second Wave* 2 (1). Reprinted in Jane Jaquette (ed.) *Women in Politics*. New York: Wiley.

Ganz, Marshall. 2000. "Resources and Resourcefulness: Strategic Capacity in the Unionization of California Agriculture," *American Journal of Sociology* 105 (4): 1003–63.

Gaventa, John. 1980. *Power and Powerlessness: Quiescence and Rebellion in an Appalachian Valley*. Urbana, IL: University of Illinois Press.

Gilens, Martin. 2012. *Affluence and Influence: Economic Inequality and Political Power in America*. New York and Princeton, NJ: Russell Sage Foundation and Princeton University Press.

Gitlin, Todd. 1980. *The Whole World Is Watching: Mass Media in the Making and Unmaking of the New Left*. Berkeley, CA: University of California Press.

Go, Julian. 2007. "The Provinciality of American Empire: 'Liberal Exceptionalism' and US Colonial Rule, 1898–1912," *Comparative Studies in Society and History* 49 (1): 74–108.

Goldstone, Jack A. 2001. "Toward a Fourth Generation of Revolutionary Theory," *Annual Review of Political Science* 4: 139–87.

Goldstone, Jack A., and Bert Useem. 1999. "Prison Riots as Microrevolutions: An Extension of State-Centered Theories of Revolution," *American Journal of Sociology* 104 (1): 985–1029.

Goodwin, Jeff. 1997. "The Libidinal Constitution of a High-Risk Social Movement: Affectual Ties and Solidarity in the Huk Rebellion, 1946 to 1954," *American Sociological Review* 62 (1): 53–69.

Gorski, Philip S. 2003. *The Disciplinary Revolution: Calvinism and the Rise of the State in Early Modern Europe*. Chicago, IL: University of Chicago Press.

Gould, Deborah B. 2009. *Moving Politics: Emotion and ACT UP's Fight Against AIDS*. Chicago, IL: University of Chicago Press.

Gould, Roger V. 1995. *Insurgent Identities: Class, Community, and Protest in Paris from 1848 to the Commune*. Chicago, IL: University of Chicago Press.

Gramsci, Antonio. 1971. *Selections from the Prison Notebooks*. New York: International Publishers.

Habermas, Jürgen. 1994. *The Structural Transformation of the Public Sphere: An Inquiry into a Category of Bourgeois Society*. Cambridge, MA: MIT Press.

Hacker, Jacob S., and Paul Pierson. 2005. *Off Center: The Republican Revolution and the Erosion of American Democracy*. New Haven, CT: Yale University Press.

Hall, Peter A., and David Soskice (eds). 2001. *Varieties of Capitalism: The Institutional Foundations of Comparative Advantage*. New York: Oxford University Press.

Halliday, Terence C., and Bruce G. Carruthers. 2007. "The Recursivity of Law: Global Norm Making and National Lawmaking in the Globalization of Corporate Insolvency Regimes," *American Journal of Sociology* 112 (4): 1135–202.

Heaney, Michael T., and Fabio Rojas. 2015. *Party in the Street: The Antiwar Movement and the Democratic Party after 9/11*. New York: Cambridge University Press.

Hirschman, Albert O. 1970. *Exit, Voice, and Loyalty: Responses to Decline in Firms, Organizations and States*. Cambridge, MA: Harvard University Press.

Igo, Sarah. 2007. *The Averaged American: Surveys, Citizens, and the Making of a Mass Public*. Cambridge, MA: Harvard University Press.

Ikegami, Eiko. 1995. *The Taming of the Samurai: Honorific Individualism and the Making of Modern Japan*. Cambridge, MA: Harvard University Press.

Jung, Wooseok, Brayden G. King, and Sarah A. Soule. 2014. "Issue Bricolage: Explaining the Configuration of the Social Movement Sector, 1960–1995," *American Journal of Sociology* 120 (1): 1–39.

Keck, Margaret E., and Kathryn Sikkink. 1998. *Activists Beyond Borders: Advocacy Networks in International Politics*. Ithaca, NY: Cornell University Press.

Keyssar, Alexander. 2000. *The Right to Vote: The Contested History of Democracy in the United States*. New York: Basic Books.

Kiser, Edgar, and April Linton. 2002. "The Hinges of History: State-Making and Revolt in Early Modern France," *American Sociological Review* 67 (6): 889–910.

Krause, Monika. 2014. *The Good Project: Humanitarian Relief NGOs and the Fragmentation of Reason*. Chicago, IL: University of Chicago Press.

Kroneberg, Clemens, and Andreas Wimmer. 2012. "Struggling over the Boundaries of Belonging: A Formal Model of Nation Building, Ethnic Closure, and Populism," *American Journal of Sociology* 118 (1): 176–230.

Lachmann, Richard. 1990. "Class Formation without Class Struggle: An Elite Conflict Theory of the Transition to Capitalism," *American Sociological Review* 55 (3): 398–414.

Lachmann, Richard. 2011. "American Patrimonialism: The Return of the Repressed," *Annals of the American Academy of Political and Social Science* 636: 204–30.

Lazarsfeld, Paul, Bernard Berelson, and Hazel Gaudet. 1944. *The People's Choice: How the Voter Makes Up His Mind in a Presidential Campaign*. New York: Columbia University Press.

Lee, Caroline W. 2015. *Do-It-Yourself Democracy: The Rise of the Public Engagement Industry*. New York: Oxford University Press.

Lee, Cheol-Sung. 2012. "Associational Networks and Welfare States in Argentina, Brazil, South Korea, and Taiwan," *World Politics* 64 (3): 507–54.

Lee, Cheol-Sung, Young-Bum Kim, and Jae-Mahn Shim. 2011. "The Limit of Equality Projects: Public Sector Expansion, Sectoral Conflicts, and Income Inequality in Postindustrial Economies," *American Sociological Review* 76 (1): 100–24.

Levitsky, Sandra. 2014. *Caring for Our Own: Why There is No Political Demand for New American Social Welfare Rights*. New York: Oxford University Press.

Lieberman, Denise. 2012. "Barriers to the Ballot Box: New Restrictions Underscore the Need for Voting Laws Enforcement," *Human Rights* 39 (1): 2–14.

Lipset, Seymour Martin, and Stein Rokkan (eds). 1967. *Party Systems and Voter Alignments: Cross-National Perspectives.* New York: Free Press.

Lukes, Steven. 1974. *Power: A Radical View.* New York: Macmillan.

Mann, Michael. 1986. *The Sources of Social Power: A History of Power from the Beginning to A.D. 1760.* New York: Cambridge University Press.

Manza, Jeff, and Christopher Uggen. 2004. "Punishment and Democracy: The Disenfranchisement of Nonincarcerated Felons in the United States," *Perspectives on Politics* 2: 491–505.

Manza, Jeff, Michael Hout, and Clem Brooks. 1995. "Class Voting in Capitalist Democracies Since World War II: Dealignment, Realignment, or Trendless Fluctuation?" *Annual Review of Sociology* 21: 137–62.

Markoff, John. 1985. "The Social Geography of Rural Revolt at the Beginning of the French Revolution," *American Sociological Review* 50 (6): 761–81.

Markoff, John. 2013. "Democracy's Past Transformations, Present Challenges, and Future Prospects," *International Journal of Sociology* 43 (2): 13–40.

Martin, Isaac. 2008. *The Permanent Tax Revolt: How the Property Tax Transformed American Politics.* Stanford, CA: Stanford University Press.

Marwell, Nicole. 2007. *Bargaining for Brooklyn: Community Organizations in the Entrepreneurial City.* Chicago, IL: University of Chicago Press.

McAdam, Doug. 1982. *Political Process and the Development of Black Insurgency, 1930–1970.* Chicago, IL: University of Chicago Press.

McAdam, Doug. 1989. "The Biographical Consequences of Activism," *American Sociological Review* 54 (5): 744–60.

McAdam, Doug, and Hilary Boudet. 2012. *Putting Social Movements in their Place: Explaining Opposition to Energy Projects in the United States, 2000–2005.* New York: Cambridge University Press.

McAdam, Doug, John D. McCarthy, and Mayer N. Zald. 1996. *Comparative Perspectives on Social Movements: Political Opportunities, Mobilizing Structures, and Cultural Framings.* New York: Cambridge University Press.

McCall, Leslie. 2005. "The Complexity of Intersectionality," *Signs* 30 (3): 1771–800.

McCarthy, John D., and Mayer N. Zald. 1977. "Resource Mobilization and Social Movements: A Partial Theory," *American Journal of Sociology* 82 (6): 1212–41.

McElwee, Sean. 2014. "Why the Voting Gap Matters," available at: http://www.demos.org/sites/default/files/publications/Voters &NonVoters.pdf (accessed December 15, 2015).

McQuarrie, Michael. 2013. "Community Organizations in the Foreclosure Crisis: The Failure of Neoliberal Civil Society," *Politics and Society* 41 (1): 73–101.

McVeigh, Rory, Daniel J. Myers, and David Sikkink. 2004. "Corn, Klansmen, and Coolidge: Structure and Framing in Social Movements," *Social Forces* 83 (2): 653–90.

Mettler, Suzanne. 2005. *Soldiers to Citizens: The G.I. Bill and the Making of the Greatest Generation.* New York: Oxford University Press.

Mettler, Suzanne. 2011. "Our Hidden Government Benefits," *New York Times*, September 19.

Mettler, Suzanne, and Joe Soss. 2004. "The Consequences of Public Policy for Democratic Citizenship: Bridging Policy Studies and Mass Politics," *Perspectives on Politics* 2 (1): 55–73.

Meyer, John W., Francisco O. Ramirez, and Yasemin Nuhoğlu Soysal. 1992. "World Expansion of a Mass Education, 1870–1980," *Sociology of Education* 65 (2): 128–49.

Meyer, John W., John Boli, and George M. Thomas. 1997. "World Society and the Nation-State," *American Journal of Sociology* 103 (1): 144–81.

Mills, C. Wright. 1956. *The Power Elite.* New York: Oxford University Press.

Mills, C. Wright. 1959. *The Sociological Imagination.* New York: Oxford University Press.

Mitchell, Timothy. 1991. "The Limits of the State: Beyond Statist Approaches and Their Critics," *American Political Science Review* 85 (1): 77–96.

Molotch, Harvey. 1976. "The City as a Growth Machine: Toward a Political Economy of Place," *American Journal of Sociology* 82 (2): 309–32.

Moore, Barrington Jr. 1966. *Social Origins of Dictatorship and Democracy: Lord and Peasant in the Making of the Modern World.* Boston, MA: Beacon Press.

Mora, G. Cristina. 2014. "Cross-Field Effects and Ethnic Classification: The Institutionalization of Hispanic Panethnicity, 1965 to 1990," *American Sociological Review* 79 (2): 183–210.

Morris, Aldon D. 1993. "Birmingham Confrontation Reconsidered: An Analysis of the Dynamics and Tactics of Mobilization," *American Sociological Review* 58 (5): 621–36.

Munson, Ziad. 2008. *The Making of Pro-Life Activists: How Social Movement Mobilization Works*. Chicago, IL: University of Chicago Press.

Nettl, J.P. 1968. "The State as a Conceptual Variable," *World Politics* 20 (4): 559–92.

Neuman, W. Russell. 1986. *The Paradox of Mass Politics: Knowledge and Opinion in the American Electorate*. Cambridge, MA: Harvard University Press.

Ojeda, Christopher, and Peter K. Hatemi. 2015. "Accounting for the Child in the Transmission of Party Identification," *American Sociological Review* 80 (6): 1150–74.

Orloff, Ann Shola. 1993. "Gender and the Social Rights of Citizenship: The Comparative Analysis of Gender Relations and Welfare States," *American Sociological Review* 58 (3): 303–28.

Orloff, Ann Shola. 2009. "Gendering the Comparative Analysis of Welfare States: An Unfinished Agenda," *Sociological Theory* 27 (3): 317–43.

Orloff, Ann Shola. 2012. "Remaking Power and Politics," *Social Science History* 36 (1): 1–21.

Padgett, John F., and Christopher K. Ansell. 1993. "Robust Action and the Rise of the Medici, 1400–1434," *American Journal of Sociology* 98 (6): 1259–319.

Page, Benjamin I., Larry M. Bartels, and Jason Seawright. 2013. "Democracy and the Policy Preferences of Wealthy Americans," *Perspectives on Politics*, 11 (1): 51–73.

Pateman, Carole. 1988. "The Patriarchal Welfare State," in Amy Gutmann (ed.) *Democracy and the Welfare State*. Princeton, NJ: Princeton University Press.

Payne, Charles M. 1995. *I've Got the Light of Freedom: The Organizing Tradition and the Mississippi Freedom Struggle*. Berkeley, CA: University of California Press.

Pfaff, Steven, and Hyojoung Kim. 2003. "Exit-Voice Dynamics in Collective Action: An Analysis of Emigration and Protest in the East German Revolution," *American Journal of Sociology* 109 (2): 401–44.

Pierson, Paul. 1994. *Dismantling the Welfare State? Reagan, Thatcher, and the Politics of Retrenchment*. Cambridge, MA: Harvard University Press.

Piven, Frances Fox, and Richard A. Cloward. 1977. *Poor People's Movements: Why They Succeed, How They Fail*. New York: Pantheon.

Piven, Frances Fox, and Richard A. Cloward. 2000. *Why Americans Still Don't Vote and Why Politicians Want It That Way*. Boston, MA: Beacon Press.

Polletta, Francesca. 2002. *Freedom is an Endless Meeting: Democracy in American Social Movements*. Chicago, IL: University of Chicago Press.

Prior, Markus. 2013. "Media and Political Polarization," *Annual Review of Political Science* 16: 101–27.

Putnam, Robert D. 2000. *Bowling Alone: The Collapse and Revival of American Community*. New York: Simon and Schuster.

Riley, Dylan. 2005. "Civic Associations and Authoritarian Regimes in Interwar Europe: Italy and Spain in Comparative Perspective," *American Sociological Review* 70 (2): 288–310.

Rosenstone, Steven J., and John Mark Hansen. 1993. *Mobilization, Participation, and Democracy in America*. New York: Macmillan.

Rousseau, Jean-Jacques. 1959. *The Social Contract and Discourses*, trans. G.D.H. Cole. New York: E.P. Dutton.

Roxborough, Ian. 1988. "Modernization Theory Revisited: A Review Article," *Comparative Studies in Society and History* 30 (4): 753–61.

Ruggie, Mary. 1984. *The State and Working Women: A Comparative Study of Britain and Sweden*. Princeton, NJ: Princeton University Press.

Ryan, Joseph W. 2012. *Samuel Stouffer and the GI Survey: Sociologists and Soldiers during the Second World War*. Austin, TX: University of Texas Press.

Sartre, Jean-Paul. 2004 [1961]. Preface to Frantz Fanon, *The Wretched of the Earth*. New York: Grove Press.

Schama, Simon. 1988. *The Embarrassment of Riches: An Interpretation of Dutch Culture in the Golden Age*. Berkeley, CA: University of California Press.

Schattschneider, E.E. 1960. *The Semisovereign People: A Realist's View of Democracy in America*. New York: Holt, Rinehart and Winston.

Scott, James C. 1987. *Weapons of the Weak: Everyday Forms of Peasant Resistance*. New Haven, CT: Yale University Press.

Scott, James C. 1998. *Seeing Like a State: How Certain Schemes to Improve the Human Condition Have Failed*. New Haven, CT: Yale University Press.

Sewell, William H. Jr. 1992. "A Theory of Structure: Duality, Agency, and Transformation," *American Journal of Sociology* 98 (1): 1–29.

Sirianni, Carmen. 2014. "Bringing the State Back In through Collaborative Governance: Emergent Mission and Practice at the US Environmental Protection Agency," in Jennifer Girouard and Carmen Sirianni (eds) *Varieties of Civic Innovation: Deliberative, Collaborative, Network, and Narrative Approaches.* Louisville, TN: Vanderbilt University Press, pp. 203–38.

Skocpol, Theda. 1976. "France, Russia, China: A Structural Analysis of Social Revolutions," *Comparative Studies in Society and History,* 18 (2): 175–210.

Skocpol, Theda. 1979. *States and Social Revolutions: A Comparative Analysis of France, Russia, and China.* New York: Cambridge University Press.

Skocpol, Theda. 1980. "Political Response to Capitalist Crisis: Neo-Marxist Theories of the State and the Case of the New Deal," *Politics and Society* 10 (2): 155–201.

Skocpol, Theda. 1985. "Bringing the State Back In: Strategies of Analysis in Current Research," in Peter Evans, Dietrich Rueschemeyer, and Theda Skocpol (eds) *Bringing the State Back In.* New York: Cambridge University Press, pp. 3–37.

Skocpol, Theda. 1992. *Protecting Soldiers and Mothers: The Political Origins of Social Policy in the United States.* Cambridge, MA: Harvard University Press.

Skocpol, Theda, and Vanessa Williamson. 2012. *The Tea Party and the Remaking of Republican Conservatism.* New York: Oxford University Press.

Slater, Dan. 2009. "Revolutions, Crackdowns, and Quiescence: Communal Elites and Democratic Mobilization in Southeast Asia," *American Journal of Sociology* 115 (1): 203–54.

Smith, Rogers. 1993. "Beyond Tocqueville, Myrdal, and Hartz: The Multiple Traditions in America," *American Political Science Review* 87 (3): 549–66.

Snow, David A., R. Burke Rochford, Steven K. Worden, and Robert D. Benford. 1986. "Frame Alignment Processes, Micromobilization, and Movement Participation," *American Sociological Review* 41 (4): 464–81.

Sohrabi, Nader. 1995. "Historicizing Revolutions: Constitutional Revolutions in the Ottoman Empire, Iran, and Russia, 1905–1908," *American Journal of Sociology* 100 (6): 1383–447.

Somers, Margaret R. 1993. "Citizenship and the Place of the Public Sphere: Law, Community, and Political Culture in the Transition to Democracy," *American Sociological Review* 58 (5): 587–620.

Soysal, Yasemin Nuhoğlu. 1994. *Limits of Citizenship: Migrants and Postnational Membership in Europe.* Chicago, IL: University of Chicago Press.

Stamatov, Peter. 2010. "Activist Religion, Empire, and the Emergence of Modern Long-Distance Advocacy Networks," *American Sociological Review* 75 (4): 607–28.

Steinmetz, George. 2014. "The Sociology of Empires, Colonies, and Postcolonialism," *Annual Review of Sociology* 40: 77–103.

Strang, David. 1990. "From Dependency to Sovereignty: An Event History Analysis of Decolonization, 1870–1987," *American Sociological Review*, 55 (6): 846–60.

Strang, David. 1992. "The Inner Incompatibility of Empire and Nation: Popular Sovereignty and Decolonization," *Sociological Perspectives* 35 (2): 367–84.

Tilly, Charles. 1992. *Coercion, Capital, and European States, AD 990–1992*. New York: Blackwell.

Tilly, Charles. 1995. *Popular Contention in Great Britain, 1758–1834*. Cambridge, MA: Harvard University Press.

Tilly, Charles. 1998. *Durable Inequality*. Berkeley, CA: University of California Press.

Traugott, Mark. 1980. "Determinants of Political Orientation: Class and Organization in the Parisian Insurrection of June 1848," *American Journal of Sociology* 86 (1): 32–49.

Tucker, Robert C. (ed.). 1978. *The Marx-Engels Reader*, 2nd edn. New York: W.W. Norton.

Uggen, Christopher, and Jeff Manza. 2002. "Democratic Contraction? Political Consequences of Felon Disenfranchisement in the United States," *American Sociological Review* 67 (6): 777–803.

Verba, Sidney, Kay Lehman Schlozman, and Henry E. Brady. 1995. *Voice and Equality: Civic Voluntarism in American Politics*. Cambridge, MA: Harvard University Press.

Viterna, Jocelyn. 2013. *Women in War: The Micro-Processes of Mobilization in El Salvador*. New York: Oxford University Press.

Vonnegut, Kurt. 1988 [1968]. "Harrison Bergeron," in *Welcome to the Monkey House*. New York: Dell.

Walder, Andrew G. 2009. *Fractured Rebellion: The Beijing Red Guard Movement*. Cambridge, MA: Harvard University Press.

Watkins, Susan Cotts. 1991. *From Provinces to Nations: Demographic Integration in Western Europe 1870–1960*. Princeton, NJ: Princeton University Press.

Watkins, Susan Cotts, Ann Swidler, and Thomas Hannan. 2012. "Outsourcing Social Transformation: Development NGOs as Organizations," *Annual Review of Sociology* 38: 285–315.

Weaver, Vesla, and Amy E. Lerman. 2010. "Political Consequences of the Carceral State," *American Political Science Review* 104 (4): 817–33.

Weber, Max. 1978 [1918–20]. *Economy and Society*. Berkeley, CA: University of California Press.

Wittfogel, Karl August. 1957. *Oriental Despotism: A Comparative Study of Total Power*. New Haven, CT: Yale University Press.

Xu, Xiaohong. 2013. "Belonging Before Believing: Group Ethos and Bloc Recruitment in the Making of Chinese Communism," *American Sociological Review* 78 (5): 773–96.

Young, Michael P. 2006. *Bearing Witness against Sin: The Evangelical Birth of the American Social Movement*. Chicago, IL: University of Chicago Press.

Zhao, Dingxin. 2001. *The Power of Tiananmen: State-Society Relations and the 1989 Beijing Student Movement*. Chicago, IL: University of Chicago Press.

Zhao, Dingxin. 2009. "The Mandate of Heaven and Performance Legitimation in Historical and Contemporary China," *American Behavioral Scientist* 53 (3): 416–33.

Index